Adopting a Pet

Our Best Friends

OUR BEST FRIENDS

Adopting a Pet

Janice Biniok

ELDORADO INK

Produced by OTTN Publishing, Stockton, New Jersey

Eldorado Ink
PO Box 100097
Pittsburgh, PA 15233
www.eldoradoink.com

CPSIA compliance information: Batch#OBF010111-1. For further information,
contact Eldorado Ink at info@eldoradoink.com.

First printing

1 3 5 7 9 8 6 4 2

Library of Congress Cataloging-in-Publication Data

Biniok, Janice.
 Adopting a pet / Janice Biniok.
    p. cm. — (Our best friends)
 Includes bibliographical references and index.
 ISBN 978-1-932904-73-4 (hardcover) — ISBN 978-1-932904-79-6 (trade)
 1. Pet adoption—Juvenile literature. I. Title.
 SF416.2.B48 2011
 636.088'7—dc22

                          2010034487

**For information about custom editions, special sales, or premiums,
please contact our special sales department at info@eldoradoink.com.**

TABLE OF CONTENTS

Introduction

GARY KORSGAARD, DVM

The mutually beneficial relationship between humans and animals began long before the dawn of recorded history. Archaeologists believe that humans began to capture and tame wild goats, sheep, and pigs more than 9,000 years ago. These animals were then bred for specific purposes, such as providing humans with a reliable source of food or providing furs and hides that could be used for clothing or the construction of dwellings.

Other animals had been sought for companionship and assistance even earlier. The dog, believed to be the first animal domesticated, began living and working with Stone Age humans in Europe more than 14,000 years ago. Some archaeologists believe that wild dogs and humans were drawn together because both hunted the same prey. By taming and training dogs, humans became more effective hunters. Dogs, meanwhile, enjoyed the social contact with humans and benefited from greater access to food and warm shelter. Dogs soon became beloved pets as well as trusted workers. This can be seen from the many artifacts depicting dogs that have been found at ancient sites in Asia, Europe, North America, and the Middle East.

The earliest domestic cats appeared in the Middle East about 5,000 years ago. Small wild cats were probably first attracted to human settlements because plenty of rodents could be found wherever harvested grain was stored. Cats played a useful role in hunting and killing these pests, and it is likely that grateful humans rewarded them for this assistance. Over time, these small cats gave up some of their aggressive wild behaviors and began living among humans. Cats eventually became so popular in ancient Egypt that they were believed to possess magical powers. Cat statues were placed outside homes to ward off evil spirits, and mummified cats were included in royal tombs to accompany their owners into the afterlife.

Today, few people believe that cats have supernatural powers, but most pet owners feel a magical bond with their pets, whether they are dogs, cats, hamsters, rabbits, horses, or parrots. The lives of pets and their people become inextricably inter-twined, providing strong emotional and physical rewards for both humans and animals. People of all ages can benefit from the loving companionship of a pet. Not surprisingly, then, pet ownership is widespread. Recent statistics indicate that about 60 percent of all households in the United States and Canada have at least one pet, while the figure is close to 50 percent of households in the United Kingdom. For millions of people, therefore, pets truly have become their "best friends."

Finding the best animal friend can be a challenge, however. Not only are there many types of domesticated pets, but each has specific needs, characteristics, and personality traits. Even within a category of pets, such as dogs, different breeds will flourish in different surroundings and with different treatment. For example, a German Shepherd may not be the right pet for a person living in a cramped urban apartment; that person might be better off caring for a smaller dog like a Toy Poodle or Shih Tzu, or perhaps a cat. On the other hand, an active person who loves the outdoors may prefer the companion-ship of a Labrador Retriever to that of a small dog or a passive indoor pet like a goldfish or hamster.

The joys of pet ownership come with certain responsibilities. Bringing a pet into your home and your neigh-borhood obligates you to care for and train the pet properly. For exam-ple, a dog must be housebroken, taught to obey your commands, and trained to behave appropriately when he encounters other people or ani-mals. Owners must also be mindful of their pet's particular nutritional and medical needs.

The purpose of the OUR BEST FRIENDS series is to provide a helpful and comprehensive introduction to pet ownership. Each book contains the basic information a prospective pet owner needs in order to choose the right pet for his or her situation and to care for that pet throughout the pet's lifetime. Training, socializa-tion, proper nutrition, potential medical issues, and the legal respon-sibilities of pet ownership are thoroughly explained and discussed, and an abundance of expert tips and suggestions are offered. Whether it is a hamster, corn snake, guinea pig, or Labrador Retriever, the books in the OUR BEST FRIENDS series provide everything the reader needs to know about how to have a happy, well-adjusted, and well-behaved pet.

> Once you open your home and heart to an adopted pet, you'll understand that adopting a pet is not just about saving an abandoned animal's life—it's about making a life together.

CHAPTER ONE

Pet Adoption

Congratulations on choosing to adopt your next animal companion! Pet adoption is one of the most sensible, economical, and socially responsible methods of acquiring a new pet. This book will help you navigate through the pet adoption process.

WHY ADOPT?

There are many reasons to adopt a homeless animal rather than to purchase a pet from a breeder or pet store. Perhaps the best reason is that adopting saves an animal's life. According to the Humane Society of the United States, animal shelters across the country euthanize between 3 million and 4 million pets every year because there aren't enough homes for them. Pet overpopulation has become a huge problem. You can become a part of the solution by taking in a homeless pet.

In addition to being a socially responsible thing to do, adoption offers practical advantages. Whatever kind of pet you could get from a breeder or pet store you can also get through adoption. But with adoption you aren't restricted to young or baby animals. You can choose from pets of all different ages. So if, for instance, you've been dreaming of a canine companion but don't want the mess and stress of housetraining a puppy, you might adopt a young adult dog that has already been trained. If you like nothing more than lounging around the house in your spare time, a senior pet might complement your laid-back lifestyle.

Another advantage to adoption is cost. Adopting a pet is usually cheaper than purchasing one, and the difference is often considerable. Plus, adoption fees may cover important veterinary care, such as vaccinations and sterilization surgery.

In many cases, animal adoption agencies offer a range of helpful services. Whether you adopt from a shelter or rescue group, the organization's staff can provide expert adoption counseling to help you locate the perfect pet. They may perform temperament tests on the pet of your choice to make sure it will get along with children or other pets in your household. They are a good source of free advice on training and behavior. They may even offer free or low-cost training classes and seminars. Such perks help ensure that adoptable animals find homes that truly last forever.

LIMITATIONS OF ADOPTION

Shelters and rescue groups provide an abundance of benefits. But the animals they place often come with some strings attached. Prospective adopters must meet certain criteria before an agency will allow an adoption to proceed. Adopters must also agree to provide a minimum stan-

dard of pet care after taking their pet home. While a few adoption agencies have earned a reputation for enforcing overly strict rules, the great majority require only what one might consider to be proper care for the health and happiness of a pet. And since that's what any responsible pet adopter wants anyway, most people don't find the requirements burdensome.

Some adoptable animals come with behavioral issues. This is hardly surprising, given the difficult circumstances many of these pets have experienced. If an animal appears extremely shy, aggressive, or unsocialized, you might want to think twice about adopting that animal, especially if you are a first-time pet owner. Keep in mind, though, that regardless of where they have come from, all pets require proper training. In many cases the training needed to make an adopted pet an excellent companion is no more extensive than the training that would be necessary for an animal obtained from a pet store or breeder.

Adopted pets often come with little or no genetic or health history. If you adopt a mixed-breed puppy, for example, there are no guarantees as to what size, temperament, or coat length the puppy will have as an adult. Without breeding records, it's impossible to predict what kind of latent genetic defects the animal may harbor. Adopting an animal with an unknown history is like opening a present. You can't be sure what's inside, but there's always a little bit of a thrill in being surprised. You could end up with something much better than you expected.

ADOPTION OPTIONS

Adopting a pet is a big step. It's important to choose the right animal, but it's just as important to choose the right adoption agency. Pet adoption has changed dramatically in the last couple decades. The community animal shelter or pound is no longer the sole source of adoptable animals. Nonprofit rescue groups, some of which specialize in specific breeds or species, have proliferated. For pet adopters, this means there are even more sources of adoptable animals. And now it's easier than ever to find the specific type of pet you desire.

PETS AND CHILDREN

A pet can greatly enrich a child's life. Not only can kids form deep emotional bonds with their pets, but they can also learn valuable life lessons, such as responsibility and the importance of treating all living creatures with respect and kindness. Bear in mind, though, that children need instruction and guidance in how to treat a pet. The following guidelines should help:

Always supervise a young child's interactions with your pet, both to ensure that the child is acting appropriately and to make certain that the pet isn't giving signs of aggressive behavior.

Monitor a child's care of a pet to make sure the child doesn't neglect pet care duties.

Be prepared to take over pet care duties if a child fails to perform them.

Encourage children to spend time with their pets or to participate in training classes, thereby allowing them to reap the most benefits from pet ownership.

ANIMAL SHELTERS: The growth in the number of rescue groups has had little effect on the success of established animal shelters. That's because shelters have unique benefits to offer. They occupy a specific location and can display many different animals for potential adopters to see. It's nice to be able to compare pets before choosing just one.

This type of adoption agency does have a few drawbacks. Shelters can be noisy, stressful places for animals. The animals don't always receive much individual attention or exercise. Under these conditions, it's hard to judge an animal's true personality, as stressed animals may appear uncharacteristically shy, aggressive, or unresponsive.

Most animal shelters are professional and trustworthy. But when looking for a pet to adopt, you should observe carefully the condition of the premises and the appearance of the animals. Some privately run shelters, especially in rural areas where sources of funding are scarce, have faced charges of cruelty for keeping animals in miserable conditions. If a shelter seems not to be providing clean living conditions and adequate food and water for its animals, you should walk away—and report the shelter to the local authorities. You don't want to adopt an unhealthy animal that may eventually cost you a broken heart.

RESCUE GROUPS: Unlike animal shelters, rescue groups don't have a central location with lots of animals on display. Rather, they operate as networks of individual foster homes,

Animal shelters often offer a range of services. They may provide training classes or pet care seminars. They may employ a professional animal behaviorist for consultation. Some even have a veterinarian on staff and offer low-cost veterinary services.

often spread over a large geographic area. Thus it may take a little more effort and mileage to meet with an adoptable pet from a rescue group. But there are advantages to adopting a pet from this type of agency.

First, keeping a pet in a home environment gives foster volunteers valuable insights to a pet's personality. Serious behavior issues such as separation anxiety in dogs, litter box aversion in cats, and aversion to handling in birds will be readily apparent. The animals tend to receive much more individual attention in this type of setting, and they may even receive some much-needed training.

Second, many rescue groups specialize in a particular breed or species, which makes finding the exact type of pet you have in mind so much easier. If you are looking for a purebred dog, a rescue group that specializes in that breed is the best place to start. If you have your heart set on getting a bunny buddy, a rabbit rescue group can help you find a match. There are bird rescue groups, reptile rescue groups, and cat rescue groups. No matter what type of pet you have a yearning to find, there is probably a rescue group that specializes in that kind of animal.

Third, specialized rescue groups are a good source of expert advice. Their volunteers are exceptionally

People who are interested in a particular type of pet often volunteer to assist groups dedicated to rescuing abandoned animals and helping them find new homes.

knowledgeable in their species or breed, and they can also provide referrals to veterinarians who are experienced in the unique needs of the animal you seek. It's obvious why rescue groups have grown and thrived. But regardless of the success of this type of adoption model, you should always evaluate a rescue group carefully before signing an adoption contract.

People who start rescue groups almost always do so with good intentions. However, good intentions

FAST FACT

Reputable shelters and rescue groups do their best to ensure that the animals they put up for adoption are in good health. However, you should still do a quick check before taking a pet home. The following signs are indicators of a possible health issue: dull skin or coat, flaking or peeling skin, cloudy or teary eyes, discharge from any orifice, lameness, lethargy, diarrhea, excessive scratching, and low body weight. If you observe any of these signs, inquire further before accepting the pet.

alone aren't enough to serve the best interests of animals. Almost anyone can start a rescue group, regardless of his or her knowledge or experience. Unlike animal shelters, rescue groups don't require a sizable capital investment. Moreover, rescue groups are unregulated. They don't have to meet minimum standards of conduct. Therefore, it's up to you to make sure that a rescue group is reputable. Always evaluate adoptable animals for health and condition, and ask plenty of questions about the organization so that you can feel confident you'll receive fair, professional treatment.

OTHER SOURCES: Nonprofit adoption agencies are by no means the only sources of adoptable animals. You might have a friend, relative, neighbor, or coworker who is seeking a new home for a pet. You might hear about a pet that needs a new home through word of mouth, a newspaper ad, or a posting on a public bulletin board. You might even find a lost animal whose owner you are unable to locate, or an animal that has obviously been abandoned.

With these types of adoption opportunities, you won't be able to draw on the support that animal shelters or rescue groups can provide. Still, an informal adoption may be worth considering. One caution: Try not to be swayed by the allure of a free pet or feelings of pity. Your decision should be based on what's good for you and for the animal.

You may find cute pets available for sale or adoption at local farms or through newspaper ads.

Make sure the pet in question is a good match for your circumstances.

FINDING AN ADOPTION AGENCY

Many animal shelters handle diverse species, from dogs and cats to lizards and bunnies. Most rescue groups, on the other hand, specialize in a certain species or breed. Regardless of which route you choose, the easiest way to find any type of animal adoption agency is to conduct a search on the petfinder.com Web site. This Web site provides a nationwide database of adoptable animals. The search function allows you to find adoption groups within whatever distance from your home you specify. The greater the area of your search, the better chance you have of finding the ideal pet.

Mixed-breed dogs are in abundant supply at many animal shelters and general rescue groups. If you're looking for a purebred dog, you'll have more luck contacting rescue groups that specialize in the breed you desire. National breed clubs, which represent the interests of their respective breeds, often provide contact information for rescue groups. You can find links to many national breed clubs on the American Kennel Club (AKC) Web site (www.akc.org).

Cats, too, are widely available for adoption through animal shelters and general rescue groups. For rescue groups that focus strictly on felines, check out the petfinder.com Web site. Purebred cat rescues are rare, but the Cat Fanciers Association (CFA) does have a breed rescue program. For information, go to www.cfainc.org.

Animal shelters often feature small mammals and birds as well, but rescue groups tend to diverge in this area. Rescue groups that handle these types of animals are specialized to meet the unique needs of the individual species. The House Rabbit Society (HRS) maintains a comprehensive list of rabbit rescue groups on its Web site (www.rabbit.org). One of the best resources for adoptable Guinea pigs (cavies) is the Web site guinealynx.com, which provides links to Guinea pig rescue organizations. The American Ferret Association (AFA) maintains a list of rescue links on its Web site (www.ferret.org).

The national organizations for other small mammals, unfortunately, do not provide adoption resources. Nonetheless, they are still a good source of information for adopters. Rat and mice lovers can visit the Web site of the American Fancy Rat and Mouse Association (AFRMA) at www.afrma.org. Gerbil lovers can check out the Web site of the

American Gerbil Society (AGS) at http://agsgerbils.org.

A list of reptile rescue links can be found at www.anapsid.org, the Web site of Melissa Kaplan's Herp Care Collection. Several online resources provide rescue links for various exotic animals. Two good ones are www.exotichobbyist.com and www.altpet.net.

Perhaps you have your heart set on getting a feathered friend to brighten your life. If this is the case, check out the Avian Welfare Coalition Web site at www.avianwelfare.org, or the Avian Web site at www.avianweb.com. When searching these sites for rescue links, take your time and investigate all the valuable information, insights, and advice the sites have to offer.

THE ADOPTION APPLICATION

After you've found a reputable adoption agency offering the type of pet you seek, you might think that the next step is to choose a pet and take it home. Unfortunately, pet adoption isn't quite that easy. To avoid impulsive adoptions and ensure that pets and people are a good match for each other, adoption agencies use an application process. The application helps the agency determine your suitability as a pet owner for the type of pet you seek.

Adoption requirements vary from one agency to another, and they also depend on the type of pet. For instance, an agency that places retired racing Greyhounds may require you to have a fenced yard, as it can be difficult or even impossible to train a Greyhound to respond reliably to a "come" command. Some pets may need a yard in order to get adequate exercise, while other pets are perfectly comfortable living in an apartment. It isn't uncommon for adoption agencies to require that apartment dwellers obtain written permission from their landlords to keep a pet. The agencies want to make sure that potential adopters can provide a suitable, permanent home for their animals.

Adoption agencies may also ask about other pets in your home. They want to be sure the pet you choose is one that will get along well with the pets you already have. They also want to be sure you're not collecting more animals than you can reasonably care for, and they may even request contact information for your veterinarian to check whether you keep your current pets up-to-date on vaccinations and other routine health care.

Don't be surprised if an animal adoption agency delves into your history as a pet owner. The agency may ask how many pets you've owned in the last several years and whether you've ever surrendered a pet to an animal welfare organization. Your history as a pet owner gives the agency a good idea of the kind of home you'll provide for an adopted animal.

Since some animals require a lot more personal attention than others, adoption agencies may ask about your job and your activities to assess whether you'll have the time to keep the pet on a regular schedule. This information helps the adoption agency match you with a pet that will fit your lifestyle.

An adoption agency will probably also inquire about other people who live in your home. The pet you choose must be appropriate for all members of your household. This is a concern especially when there are children or elderly persons in the home. Everyone should be receptive to adding an animal to your living situation, whether or not they will be involved in the animal's care.

Lastly, an adoption agency may require several personal references. Don't be offended by this. It's a sad fact that some people attempt to adopt animals for nefarious reasons. For example, kittens and young dogs sometimes become "bait" animals for illegal dog-fighting activities. If an adoption agency intrudes a little into

There are a number of groups that rescue unwanted racing greyhounds. In the past, these dogs were put down when they were no longer able to race. Rescued greyhounds make good pets: quiet, gentle, and loyal.

your personal life, be thankful that the agency cares enough to do so.

In addition to evaluating potential adopters carefully, many adoption agencies have in place further policies designed to prevent impulsive or inappropriate adoptions. Some agencies require a 24- or 48-hour waiting period before a pet can be taken home. This gives people a chance to change their minds if they decide they're not fully prepared to adopt a new pet. Some agencies don't permit the adoption of pets during the Christmas season. This is to prevent people from giving pets as gifts, which may or may not be wanted by

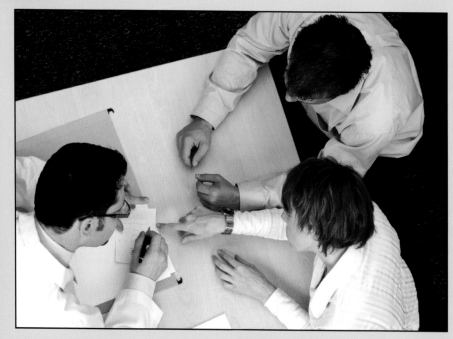

When you visit an animal shelter, breed rescue organization, or pet adoption agency, a worker will provide information about pet care and training. You'll probably also be asked to fill out a detailed application, and may be interviewed before you're permitted to take home the pet you want.

the recipients. Similarly, many agencies suspend the adoption of rabbits during the Easter season, when people tend to adopt bunnies as cute seasonal accessories.

Adoption requirements and policies vary. Even though most requirements exist to ensure the future welfare of the animals, some adoption agencies have a reputation for making it more difficult to adopt a pet than it is to adopt a child. You might be uncomfortable with practices such as home inspections before an adoption can proceed, and follow-up visits for a year afterward. Before using the services of any pet adoption agency, make sure you're aware of all its rules and requirements. If an

agency seems excessively intrusive, you'd be well served to find another agency.

THE ADOPTION CONTRACT

Adoption agencies address their post-adoption requirements in an adoption contract. This document outlines the care you are required to provide for your adopted animal as well as the requirements for any change in the animal's ownership. Conditions you may find in an adoption contract include:

A SPAY-NEUTER REQUIREMENT. This obligates you to have your pet spayed or neutered by a certain age if the animal hasn't already been sterilized.

HEALTH CARE. You may be required to provide annual veterinary check-ups, vaccinations, and heartworm preventatives for your adopted pet.

LIVING ACCOMMODATIONS. You may be required to keep your pet as an indoor pet.

CARE. Some adoption agencies, especially those for exotic animals, may specify the type of food, environment, grooming, or other special care they expect you to provide.

TRANSFER OF OWNERSHIP. If, for whatever reason, you are unable to keep your pet, some adoption contracts require you to return the animal to the adoption agency. Other contracts simply require you to notify the adoption agency in the event you are finding a new home for your pet, so that representatives of the agency can meet with the new owners.

ADDRESS CHANGE NOTIFICATION. In the interest of ensuring lifelong security for an animal, you may be required to notify the adoption agency whenever you move.

TRAINING. Some adoption contracts require you to enroll your new pet in training classes within a certain period of time after the adoption. This

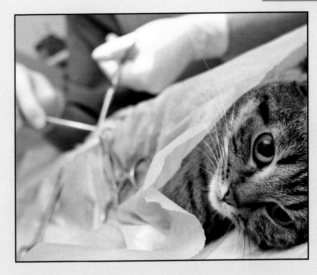

It is likely that you'll be required to spay or neuter any pet that you adopt.

is especially common with agencies that handle large, independent-minded dog breeds.

It's easy to get in the habit of neglecting to read the fine print on documents. Few people bother to read every word on their credit card agreements, bank loans, insurance policies, or mortgages. But the adoption contract is not one to be skimmed. Make sure you understand all the conditions of the contract. Ask questions if you don't. If, for any reason, you are uncomfortable with the requirements of the contract, it's best to postpone adopting a pet until you've had a chance to carefully consider the commitment you must make.

ADOPTION FEES

How much you pay to adopt your pet will depend on various factors. Obviously, you can expect to pay a lot more if you're adopting a pure-bred dog or a large parrot than if you're adopting a gerbil. Many animal shelters have fee scales that include higher fees for younger animals and lower fees for older or hard-to-place animals. Some agencies offer a discount if you adopt more than one animal. Others offer special adoption fees certain times of the year to help relieve shelter over-crowding. This is particularly true in the spring, which shelter workers often refer to as "kitten season."

Adoption fees tend to be slightly higher with rescue groups than with shelters. Some rescue groups use a fee schedule. Others set fees on a case-by-case basis. If a particular animal has required expensive veterinary treatment, for instance, the adoption fee may be higher.

THE BEST TIME TO ADOPT

As with so many of life's decisions, timing is important when adopting a pet. Even people who really love animals might not currently be in a position to provide a stable home. For instance, a student who will be heading off to college in a few months should probably not adopt a high-maintenance pet, particularly if the student's parents aren't enthusiastic about assuming pet care duties. Similarly, a couple with a newborn might be well advised to wait a while before bringing a new puppy or kitten into the household. Caring for an infant is challenging enough.

Even if your current life situation is conducive to adopting a pet, it's best to bring your new animal companion home when you have some extra time to devote to the transition. A week off work is ideal if you're adopting a dog, cat, or bird. If you can't get that much time off, plan to bring your new dog, cat, or bird home before a long weekend. With other kinds of animals, a weekend may suffice for getting your new pet situated.

Another consideration in choosing the right time to adopt is the size of the homeless-animal population in your area. Shelter populations wax and wane according to the reproductive cycles of animals. Populations also spike during natural disasters.

There are many good reasons to search for your new pet when shelter populations are at a peak. You'll find a larger variety of pets from which to choose. Also, this can be the most economical time to adopt, as many shelters offer special deals to help relieve overcrowding. Perhaps most important, high shelter populations indicate the greatest need for adoptions. This is a time when you can make the biggest difference. Contact the shelters in your area to ask about their current adoption situations. They'll be able to advise you when a new influx of animals is expected.

CHOOSING THE RIGHT PET

Adopting a pet is like becoming a parent. Your new pet will rely on you for all of its needs. Although things like food, water, and shelter are obvious necessities, some pets need a great deal more. Some pets require more stability and security than oth-

ers. Some require a lot of exercise, while others are fine with an occasional workout. Some can thrive despite minimal interaction with you, whereas others won't be happy unless they have your constant companionship. In deciding what kind of pet is right for you, think about your lifestyle. Do you have the time and energy to give a particular pet everything it needs?

PHYSICAL NEEDS: Obviously, all animals need food to survive. Yet simply making sure your pet has enough food isn't always enough. Some pets need a regular feeding schedule to develop a sense of security.

WHICH PET IS RIGHT FOR YOU?

Pet	Health Care Expenses	Exercise Needs	Companionship Demands	Training Needs	Grooming Requirements	Cleanup Needs
Dog	High	Moderate/high	Moderate/high	High	Moderate/high	High
Cat	High	Moderate	Moderate	Moderate	Moderate/high	High
Rabbit	Moderate	Moderate	Moderate	Moderate	Low/high	High
Guinea Pig	Low	Low/moderate	Moderate	Low	Low/high	High
Chinchilla	Low	Low	Low/moderate	Low	Low	High
Small Rodent	Low	Low	Low	Low	Low	Moderate
Parrot	Moderate	Moderate	Moderate/high	Moderate	Low	High
Small Birds	Low	Low	Low	Low	Low	Moderate
Reptile	Low	Low	Low	Low	Low	Low

A small pet with low care requirements, such as a hamster, could be ideal for someone who will not be home during the day or doesn't have much time to spend exercising and grooming a pet.

If your job requires odd hours or late meetings, you might want to choose a pet that does well with "free feeding." In this feeding method, the food is always available, and the pet eats when it chooses. All you have to do is make sure you periodically replenish the food source. Some small mammals, birds, and reptiles do well with free feeding.

Your pet will also require an appropriate shelter. In some cases, this means you will need to provide the right type of cage with the right type of furnishings for your particular species of pet. In other cases, it means you'll have to make adjustments to your own living space to accommodate your pet. Both situations demand indoor space. Do you have enough room to provide the right habitat for the animal you'd like to adopt?

All animals also require some type of exercise to stay healthy. Some animals can get plenty of exercise scampering about their enclosures. Others require out-of-cage playtime. Still others need outdoor exercise opportunities, which means that you, too, will have to go out to supervise. Do you have the space and the time to meet the exercise requirements of the kind of pet you want?

Grooming is another physical requirement for pets. The amount of grooming a particular pet needs will depend on the species as well as the breed. Long-haired breeds demand much more attention than short-haired breeds, regardless of whether the species in question is a dog, cat, rabbit, or Guinea pig. Keep this in mind when determining how much time you have to devote to an animal's upkeep.

Lastly, animals require veterinary care to maintain their good health. For some pets, veterinary care consists of annual checkups, vaccinations, and neuter or spay surgery, the costs of which can be significant. Other pets require much less veterinary attention. When choosing a pet, always consider the cost of health care and whether or not you can afford this financial responsibility.

EMOTIONAL NEEDS: Yes, pets have feelings, too! Meeting your pet's emotional needs can keep your pet happy, and there are many benefits to having a happy pet. Happy pets are healthy pets. They are less likely to develop destructive, annoying, or dangerous habits. If you want a pet with a good attitude and good behavior, consider how you will fulfill the emotional needs of the pet you desire.

Companionship is a very strong emotional need in many animal species. Although some species are quite independent, the real question is this: Why would you want a pet if you didn't plan to spend some time with it? All pets—even lizards and snakes—benefit from some one-on-one time with their owners. How much time can you spend with your pet buddy?

Be aware of your pet's emotional needs. Frequent handling keeps pets tame and contributes to a strong bond between pets and their people.

Besides human companionship, many animals appreciate the companionship of their own kind. Compatible animals make great playmates and provide each other with a sense of security and belonging—not to mention the entertainment they supply their owners. If you are thinking about adopting more than one pet, make sure you can afford to multiply your pet-keeping expenses.

The emotional needs of pets are rooted in their instincts. When a pet doesn't have the opportunity to fulfill its instincts, problems for both the pet and its owner result. This is why it's important to provide scratching materials for cats, chew toys for dogs, and hiding places for prey animals like rabbits, Guinea pigs, and mice. Dogs need walks, cats need high perches to observe the world, and chameleons need branches to climb.

Become familiar with the instincts of a particular type of pet in order to determine whether or not you can meet that pet's emotional needs.

HOUSEHOLD ENVIRONMENT: Whether or not you can meet the physical and emotional needs of a pet may depend on the type of household environment you can provide. Make sure your home offers a safe, secure refuge. Bringing a new cat into a home with a cat-chasing dog isn't fair to either animal. Bringing a small bird or rodent into a house with a predatory cat is sure to cause damaging stress to the tiny prey animal. Always consider your existing pets when attempting to integrate a new pet into your household.

For baby animals like puppies and kittens, safety and security must come through constant supervision.

PLAN FOR YOUR PET'S FUTURE

Before you adopt an animal, ask yourself the following questions:
- What will happen to your pet if you have to move?
- What will happen to your pet if you get married or have a child?
- Who will care for your pet in the event you can't do so any longer?
- Who will take care of your pet if you die?

Planning for contingencies such as these can help ensure your pet is well cared for, come what may.

Of all the pet choices available, these require the greatest investment of time and effort. Are you willing to make some changes to your lifestyle in order to meet the high demands of raising a baby animal?

Perhaps the youngsters in your home aren't of the animal type. There are a few things you need to consider if there are children living in your home. Children under the age of five don't always understand that their actions can cause pain and suffering to animals. This doesn't mean they can't have pets, but it does mean they require very close supervision. It can be stressful to keep a close eye on active young children in order to prevent conflicts with pets. Are you up for the challenge?

Some animals, especially small, fragile ones, aren't appropriate for households with young children. Older children may not require quite as much monitoring, but they still need adult guidance to ensure their interactions with pets are appropriate. Always be especially selective about the temperament of an animal that will be a companion for children.

LAWS AND RESTRICTIONS

Pet ownership is not an inalienable right. Many communities have laws and ordinances regarding the number and type of pets that residents may keep. It is not uncommon for communities to restrict or ban the ownership of certain exotic animals, such as large snakes or lizards. It is also becoming more common for communities to ban certain breeds of dog that are considered potentially dangerous. Some communities place limits on the number of dogs or cats you may own.

It's best to find out about relevant laws and ordinances in your community before you adopt a pet. For exotic species, you may want to consult with your local health department to find out about any restrictions or special permits that might be required.

If you rent an apartment or house, remember that landlords have the right to restrict pet ownership on their properties as they see fit. Always get approval from your landlord before you acquire a pet.

❧❧❧❧

Adopting a pet can be an extremely rewarding experience. Many adopted pets seem to sense that their owners have rescued them, and their gratitude is evident in the exceptionally strong bond they develop with their humans. By choosing adoption, you have the opportunity to enjoy the best that pet ownership has to offer.

CHAPTER TWO

Adopting a Dog

Dogs make delightful companions. They have an exceptionally strong affinity for humans, they are eager to please, and they rate quite high on the "hug-ability" scale. But they are also high maintenance. If you've determined that your lifestyle can accommodate the demands of dog ownership, you can look forward to many adventures and a whole lot of love. But what kind of dog would be the best fit for you? What kind of dog would complement your personality and integrate comfortably into your household? By choosing the right dog, you can make the human-canine bond even more rewarding.

According to the Humane Society, today there are more than 77 million pet dogs in the United States. Nearly 40 percent of all American households include at least one dog.

CHOOSING THE RIGHT DOG

Purebred dogs have certain predictable physical and temperamental characteristics. For example, Great Danes are quite large and Chihuahuas quite small. Boston Terriers are easygoing by nature, whereas Shelties tend to be a bit high strung. Knowing the characteristics of a particular breed can give you a pretty good idea of whether a purebred dog that's up for adoption would make a good match for you.

However, the majority of dogs available for adoption from shelters and rescue groups are mixed-breed animals. Mixed-breed dogs, or mutts, can possess a rich mixture of characteristics that make them highly distinctive. In some cases, a mutt's physical appearance provides clues to its genetic history. In other cases, the dog's ancestry is anyone's guess. Because of this, it can be difficult to predict what a mixed-breed dog's temperament will be like. In the case of a mixed-breed puppy, it's sometimes even hard to say how large the animal will be at adulthood.

Perhaps the best way to decide which dog is ideal for you would be to consider individual traits. Before meeting dogs in person, think about the characteristics that appeal to you the most. You might even want to rank canine characteristics in order of importance. Which are at the top of your list? Which might you be willing to forgo if a potential adoptee is a good fit in other ways?

PHYSICAL CHARACTERISTICS: Size is a major consideration when it comes to dogs. Dogs come in packages smaller than a lunchbox and larger than a cedar chest. Do you have room for a big dog? Don't forget that space isn't the only consideration. Big dogs have big food expenses, big veterinary expenses, and big doggy beds that can cover half the bedroom floor. They can knock down little kids with a single wag of their tails. Big dogs are big fun—if you are fully prepared for their bigness!

Tiny dogs have their own limitations. They can easily suffer injuries at the hands of young children. Some

FAST FACT

Dogs have an innate sense of social hierarchy. To feel secure, they need to know their place in the pack. In order to train your dog successfully, you must assume the role of pack leader. This requires you to be assertive and firm and to set limits and boundaries for your canine buddy.

Before adopting a dog, think about whether a large breed or smaller breed would be the best match for your family.

resort to nipping in order to defend themselves. Tiny dogs are best for households with older children and adults.

Fortunately, there are plenty of sizes in between the two extremes. Keep a size range in mind that will work best for your particular situation.

Hair type is another important consideration. You might be attracted to dogs with long, silky locks. But such beauty comes with high maintenance requirements. You'll need to brush the dog's coat frequently to keep it from matting. You'll also have to endure the giant dust bunnies that will infiltrate your house during the spring and fall shedding seasons.

If you have a craving for a curly-coifed canine, be prepared to do more than brushing. Curly hair often grows continuously, which means it requires trimming every couple months. If you don't want to do this yourself, you'll have to pay a professional groomer. This can add considerable expense to dog keeping. On the other hand, many curly-haired dogs don't shed much, which for you may more than justify the additional cost of grooming.

The next best thing to a low-shed dog is a short-haired dog. Dogs that have short, close-fitting coats with little or no undercoat tend to make clean house pets and require little grooming. However, this type of coat is not without its drawbacks. Short-haired dogs are prone to skin injuries and calluses. They are also less tolerant of temperature extremes.

PERSONALITY AND TEMPERAMENT: While physical characteristics are important, the personality of the dog you choose is a far better predictor of whether you'll enjoy a fulfilling relationship with your adopted pooch. Prey drive, energy level, and dependence are personality traits that come in varying degrees in the canine species. These traits can have a profound effect on how well certain dogs and certain people get along.

As predators, dogs always have a desire to chase things that move. However, this prey drive is much stronger in some dogs than in others. Dogs with a high prey drive often make excellent pets for people who wish to participate in active dog sports, such as agility or tracking, because the drive to pursue prey is easy to channel into a sporting drive. But dogs with high prey drive can have little self-control when it comes to leaving the pet cat alone or chasing after squirrels. They may not be appropriate for homes that have cats, rabbits, or rodents as pets.

FAST FACT

First-time dog owners are not advised to adopt an animal that displays extreme fearfulness, nervousness, or aggression. Inexperienced handling can make these problems worse. A dog that appears mildly shy or nervous, on the other hand, might well make a fabulous pet after placement in a stable home.

High-energy dogs can present their own challenges. Some high-energy breeds, like Border Collies, Australian Shepherds, and Doberman Pinschers, are quite popular because they are also highly intelligent. Unfortunately, some

Consider the energy level of the dog that you are thinking about adopting. High-energy breeds will need a safe place to run and plenty of opportunities for exercise to achieve maximum health and happiness.

people simply don't have the time to provide enough exercise and stimulation to keep such dogs happy. If you want a jogging companion, a dog sport partner, or a canine pal to join you in traveling, boating, or other activities, by all means find a dog that can keep up with your active lifestyle. But if you prefer quiet evenings at home and would like a couch buddy to keep you company, search for a calmer canine.

Energy level isn't the only characteristic that determines how demanding a dog will be. Certain dogs are naturally more dependent than others. Some of the toy and herding breeds thrive on human attention

BREED-GROUP TRAITS

Like people, dogs have unique personalities. But knowing a dog's breed can give you a pretty good idea of what kind of disposition that dog will have. The following outlines temperamental characteristics of the breed groups recognized by the American Kennel Club:

Terrier. Often said to be "small dogs with big attitudes," members of the Terrier group tend to be feisty and indomitable. Most require plenty of exercise and attention. Their happy attitudes and zest for life can be infectious. Terriers may not get along well with cats or small animals because of their high prey drive. Terriers also have a propensity to dig, a vestige of their ancestry as rodent eradicators.

Working. Humans developed these dogs for a variety of jobs, including sledding, guarding, and police work. Members of the Working group—including such breeds as the Rottweiler, Doberman Pinscher, Boxer, and Alaskan Malamute—tend to be independent minded. Nevertheless, with firm, consistent handling they will develop a very strong loyalty to their owners.

Herding. The traits that make members of the Herding group adept at controlling livestock also endear them to their owners. Herding breeds such as the Border Collie, Bouvier des Flandres, German Shepherd, and Shetland Sheepdog are easy to train and have a strong desire to please. On the downside, they tend to be extremely high energy and demand lots of exercise and mental stimulation.

Sporting. Originally bred to help hunters, members of the Sporting group—including the Pointer, Cocker Spaniel and other spaniels, Golden Retriever, Labrador

and tend to "shadow" their owners everywhere. This isn't necessarily a bad thing, as dependent dogs are very attentive to their owners. If you like a dog that is interested in and wants to be a part of everything you do, a dependent dog may be for you. But if you are much too busy to meet the demands of a "needy" dog,

a less dependent canine may fit better into the scheme of your life.

There is a difference between "less dependent" and "independent." Dogs are less dependent because they are naturally calm and laid back. They go with the flow and will patiently wait until you have time for them. Other dogs are independent,

Retriever, and Irish Setter—have a strong affinity for humans. Many dogs in this group make excellent family companions, as they tend to get along well with children and are easy to train. These dogs love to use their noses. Most require a lot of exercise, though.

Hound. Hounds such as the Beagle, Black and Tan Coonhound, and Greyhound were developed for hunting in packs. Because of this, they tend to get along well with other dogs, though they may have an independent streak when it comes to humans. Still, they can make excellent family dogs because they tend to spread their loyalty among family members rather than attaching themselves to one person. They can, however, be a little more challenging to train than other breed groups. Like Sporting dogs, they appreciate having opportunities to use their noses and to run.

Toy. Most toy dogs, such as the Maltese, Pomeranian, and Yorkshire Terrier—were bred for one reason: companionship. As

close companions, they can be very people-oriented and sensitive to human emotions. Since they descend from so many different backgrounds—terriers, hunting dogs, watch-dogs, and sled dogs—different members of this group have different types of personalities. Some are quite independent, whereas others are quite "needy." In general, their size makes them inappropriate pets for young children, but they are a convenient size for pet owners who travel a lot and like to take their dogs with them.

Non-sporting. The Non-sporting group includes a diverse collection of breeds that do not appear to fit comfortably in any of the other groups. They include the Dalmatian, Boston Terrier, Bulldog, and Llasa Apso. Some of these breeds were developed as companions. Some were bred for specialized hunting or other unique purposes. Each breed in this group has its own individual characteristics. If you can't find what you're looking for in one of the other breed groups, the Non-sporting group may have something to offer.

which means they have their own mind and like to use it. Some herding and working breeds, like German Shepherds, Dobermans, and Rottweilers, fall into the latter category. Although their independent streak makes these dogs great for personal protection, police work, and military work, these dogs can present major challenges for people with less assertive personalities. They require firm, consistent leadership, and some experts don't recommend these breeds (or dogs mixed with them) for first-time dog owners.

A properly sized crate will provide enough room for your dog to stand, turn around, and lie down comfortably.

PREPARING FOR YOUR NEW DOG

When you adopt a furry bundle of love, it is a time of excitement, anticipation, and maybe even a little trepidation. How will your new dog react to his new home? What kinds of challenges will you face? There are a lot of uncertainties when adopting a pet dog, but you can eliminate many of them by simply being prepared.

SUPPLIES: Many shelters and rescue groups require a waiting period of 24 to 48 hours after adoption before you can bring your new dog home. Why not use this time to pick up the supplies you'll need to care for your new pet? The vast array of pet supplies on the market makes shopping for a new dog more fun than ever. But there are a few pointers to keep in mind.

Take a shopping list with you. You'll need to purchase quite a few items, and having to run out at the last minute to pick up something you forgot can be quite annoying. You'll need a collar, a leash, food and water bowls, dog food, dog toys, dog treats, a dog crate or bed, a pooper scooper or waste bags, and whatever grooming tools your particular dog requires.

Don't sacrifice practicality for style. Purchase food and water bowls that are unbreakable and dishwasher safe. Look for dog beds and crate pads that are machine washable and easy to keep clean. Search for dog toys that are durable and well made. You'll be much happier with your purchases if you can get a lot of mileage out of them.

The crate can be a very important tool for transporting, confining, and housetraining your dog. However, in order for it to work properly, the crate needs to be the right size. If it's too large, your dog may use a portion of it to relieve himself. If it is too small, your dog will be cramped and uncomfortable.

MAKING YOUR HOME SAFE: During your dog's first few weeks at home, you should observe him closely. Pay attention to the kinds of inappropriate things or places that attract him. Remove or cover electrical cords to prevent your dog from getting into the habit of chewing on them. If your new dog likes to play among the cords behind your electronics,

block the area off with a strategically placed table or a piece of cardboard.

Dogs are natural scavengers, and they occasionally consume things that humans would consider disgusting. Their lack of good taste makes it essential to keep toxic items out of their reach. Make household cleaning products, detergents, garbage cans, medicines, pesticides, paints, and solvents completely inaccessible. Move potentially toxic houseplants out of reach. Choose a safe spot to store antifreeze, and clean up antifreeze spills immediately, as this highly poisonous substance has a sweet taste that attracts animals.

Until you find out what types of inappropriate items attract your dog, it's best to keep your floors clutter free. Dogs have been known to eat socks, slippers, and yes, even children's homework. If you have a craft or hobby room full of potentially dangerous or breakable items, close the door or gate off that area.

Dog toys make good stress relievers for a pooch that is adjusting to a new home. Offer your new dog toys of different types and with different textures so you can find out what he likes the most.

FAST FACT

Many shelter and rescue dogs haven't gotten a lot of opportunities to socialize with people or other animals. Introduce your adopted dog to new activities slowly. Give him opportunities to socialize on his own terms.

Removing temptations from your dog's environment makes life easier for you and your curious canine.

LIVING ARRANGEMENTS: Put yourself in your dog's paws. If you had to move into a new home with a new family, would you feel very comfortable if no one had thought about where you were going to eat or sleep? How would you feel if people kept moving your bed to another room every night or fed you in a different corner of the kitchen every day? Put plenty of thought into where your dog will eat and sleep to minimize change and stress.

Most dogs prefer to sleep near their human pack members, so a dog bed or crate next to your own bed is often the best choice. If you want to allow your dog to sleep on your bed, that's your personal choice. Keep in mind, however, that once you allow your dog on your bed, he'll assume

that this is his rightful place for grabbing some shut-eye. You might discover that you can't get a good night's sleep with your dog sharing the bed, or that you don't like dog hair on your pillow, but you'll have no way of explaining that to your canine buddy. He'll be confused and upset when you make him sleep somewhere else. So consider carefully whether you want to risk that ordeal by letting him sleep in your bed in the first place.

Choose a spot to feed your dog that is easy to keep clean and gives your dog a quiet place to dine. Your new dog shouldn't have to endure people bumping into him. Nor should he have to compete with other pets for food. If there are conflicts with other pets at feeding time, it may be necessary to feed them separately in their crates.

You also need to choose a designated outdoor area for your dog to do his duty. This is important because establishing a specific area for this purpose is instrumental in housetraining your dog. With consistent use of the same area, your dog will soon learn where his toilet is located.

CARING FOR YOUR DOG

Caring for a dog can be a lot of work. But it is also highly rewarding and will help you build a strong bond with your canine buddy. Allow yourself to enjoy his reactions to the care you provide. Watch how thrilled he becomes at feeding time. Bask in his quiet pleasure when you groom him. And remember—"exercise" is just another word for "play."

FEEDING: Dogs don't care if their food is healthful, but you should. The quality of the food you give your dog has a profound effect on his appearance, health, and longevity. Still, the best-quality food can easily become unhealthful through poor feeding practices. It pays to be concerned about both what you feed your dog and how you feed him.

Meat-based protein is the mainstay of a healthy dog's diet. Good-quality commercial dog foods will always list meat—such as beef, chicken, or turkey—first on the ingredients list. If the first ingredient is a meat by-product or a meal (grain product), you can assume the food is not a quality diet. Quality dog foods also contain natural forms of preservatives, such as vitamin E (sometimes listed as "mixed tocopherols") and vitamin C. Foods that contain artificial preservatives, such as BHT, BHA, and ethoxyquin, are undesirable. These characteristics of quality are the same for adult as well as puppy foods.

Your dog relies entirely on you to make good choices for him. He also depends on you to make sure he doesn't eat too much or ruin his diet with a lot of "junk food." The best way to control your dog's eating habits is to keep him on a regular feeding schedule. Feed an adult dog

Sturdy food and water bowls made of metal or ceramic are a better option than plastic dishes. Although plastic bowls are cheaper, they are harder to keep bacteria-free and easier to knock over. In addition, your dog is likely to chew a plastic dish apart over time.

twice per day. Feed a puppy three or four times per day.

Your dog's feeding schedule influences his entire biological system. It affects his patterns of elimination, his sleeping habits, and his spurts of energy. If you want to be able to predict when your dog will have to relieve himself, which is very helpful during housetraining, keep him on a regular feeding schedule. A regular feeding schedule will also help your dog sleep at night. Avoid leaving food out for your dog to snack on during the day, as this will sabotage these benefits.

A good-quality commercial dog food has all the vitamins and supplements your dog needs to be healthy. But don't give your dog too much of a good thing. Measure the amount of food you give your dog at each feeding, and adjust the amount if your dog appears to be getting too thin or too heavy.

A dog's balanced diet can easily become unbalanced with meal enhancements, snacks, and treats. There is nothing wrong with giving your dog a special treat now and then, but be sure to limit his consumption of people food, consumable chew products, and training treats. Obesity has become just as widespread among dogs as it is among people.

GROOMING: Grooming requirements will depend on your particular dog's physical characteristics. But regardless of whether your dog has a high-maintenance or low-maintenance

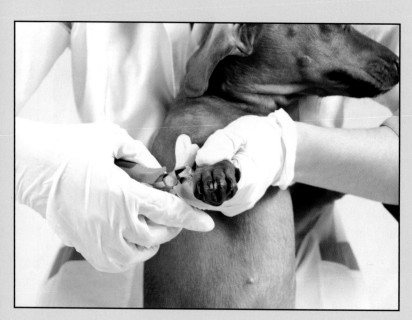

The best way to trim a dog's nails is to hold him in your lap, steady his paw, and clip off the very tips of the nails. Don't trim too far back or you'll hit the quick, or blood supply to the nail, which will cause bleeding and pain. Speaking to your dog in a soothing voice throughout the procedure will help put him at ease. Nail trimming can be traumatic, so when you're finished, give your dog a treat and lots of praise.

coat, you should groom him on a regular basis. Brushing is good for your dog's skin and coat condition. It helps your dog become accustomed to having his various body parts handled. It's also a good bonding activity.

All dogs can benefit from brushing at least once a week. Some may require more frequent attention, especially during spring and fall shedding seasons. Some curly-haired or long-haired dogs need a trim every two months. Some dogs require baths just as often. Prepare for the unique grooming needs of your dog, and purchase the appropriate tools to manage your dog's hair type.

In addition to hair care, your dog will need to have his nails trimmed every three to four weeks, his teeth brushed once or twice a week, and his ears inspected every week. All of these grooming procedures help keep your dog in good condition. If you are uncomfortable taking care of these grooming duties yourself, you'll need to find a professional dog groomer.

EXERCISING: The possibilities for getting your dog the exercise he needs are almost endless. Find an activity that both of you enjoy, and let the fun begin.

There is one activity, however, that should be on your daily to-do list: dog walking. This provides more

Before adopting, be aware of the grooming requirements of the dog that you want. All dogs need regular brushing to look their best, but some breeds, like this Yorkshire Terrier, require more in-depth coat care.

than just exercise. It provides very important social opportunities for your dog. It provides training opportunities. And it helps to satisfy your dog's need to explore and do some sniffing. Dogs that enjoy regular walks are in better physical shape, have better social skills, and tend to have fewer behavioral issues than dogs that don't go for regular walks.

Daily walks can be fun for you and your dog. As a general rule, most dogs need at least two 20-minute walks each day, plus an opportunity to run off-leash, for optimum health.

As important as it is to walk your dog, this activity doesn't fulfill all of your dog's exercise requirements. Like people, dogs benefit from a good cardiovascular workout. They need to run! A game of fetch, an obstacle course, or a good romp with some canine buddies can give your dog a heart-pumping workout.

Depending on your particular dog's energy level, you may need to spend anywhere from 30 minutes to an hour a day on canine exercise.

Exercise is one of the greatest demands of dog ownership. But then, exercising your dog is just as good for your health as it is for your dog's health. It should come as no surprise that dog owners tend to be healthier than people who don't have a canine companion.

TRAINING YOUR DOG

Many adopted dogs come with less-than-adequate training. In most cases this has less to do with the dog's potential to learn than with the previous owner's failure to invest enough time in training. Your adopted dog may not be a blank slate, but he is a slate nonetheless. Remember—he wants to please you. Help him do so by establishing good habits and behaviors from the get-go.

HOUSETRAINING: Your adopted dog may or may not have had some housetraining. Even if he has, it's not unusual for a newly adopted dog to have a few accidents when adjusting to a new environment and schedule. It's important to prevent accidents so your dog doesn't get into the bad habit of soiling your house.

For the best housetraining results, you should supervise your dog closely when you are able and keep him confined when you are not. When super-

vising your dog, watch for signs that he is looking for a place to relieve himself, like sniffing the floor and circling back and forth. If you see those signs, immediately rush him outside to his potty area. When you can't be around to monitor your dog, put him in a crate or exercise pen, or use gates to confine him to a small area of the house. Dogs don't like to eliminate where they eat or sleep, so your adopted pooch will do his best to wait until you take him outside to use the potty.

There are certain times of the day when you should anticipate your dog's need to eliminate. Make a habit of taking him outside when he's done eating, sleeping, or exercising, as all of these activities stimulate a dog's digestive system. If your dog is on a regular schedule for these

When you're walking your dog in a public area, take a plastic bag so that you can clean up after he's eliminated.

Obedience training involves more than just teaching your dog a few tricks. It should be the foundation for every activity you might do with your dog and will help to keep him safe in public.

If you want to speed up the housetraining process, praise your dog and give him a treat each time he uses his special potty spot. Ignore accidents and clean them up without a fuss, because punishing a dog that hasn't yet learned where to potty is not fair or productive. Use an enzymatic cleaner to remove the scents where accidents have occurred so your dog isn't tempted to use the same spots again. With a consistent schedule and rewards for good behavior, your adopted dog will soon respect the floors in your home.

MANNERS: It's perfectly natural for dogs to pull on leashes, rush out doors, and knock their humans down in their hurry to get at food during mealtimes. After all, humans can be so slow, there are many exciting things outside, and competing for food is a canine survival instinct. Nevertheless, such behaviors aren't the mark of a good canine companion. It's up to you to teach your dog that these behaviors are unacceptable in the human world. Insist on good manners from the start, because once your dog has established a pattern of behavior, it can be difficult to break.

activities, he'll be on a regular potty schedule, too. This is very important, because taking your dog out at the same times every day allows him to anticipate when the next potty break will be.

Have a designated potty area. This will provide a number of advantages. The scents in a used potty area will help stimulate your dog to eliminate, and he will quickly learn what he is supposed to do when you take him there. Best of all, a designated potty area makes cleaning up after your dog much easier.

Teach your dog how to walk nicely on a leash by abruptly turning and walking in the opposite direction whenever he pulls. You may not get very far on your first few walks, but that's the point. Your dog will soon learn that he gets nowhere by pulling. Providing a verbal warning cue just before executing your about-face will help your dog associate the pulling with the consequence.

Teaching good manners some-times entails replacing an undesir-able behavior with an acceptable one. If your dog has a tendency to jump up on people, make him sit for greetings. If he runs you over to get at his food, make him sit and wait while you place his bowl on the floor. When you're ready, give him permis-sion to eat his meal by saying, "OK." Similarly, train him never to go out the door until you have released him with an "OK." Good manners are simply habits developed through consistent practice. Think about what kind of manners you want your adopted dog to have, and enforce them from the first day you bring him home.

OBEDIENCE: Basic obedience train-ing is the ABC's of dog training. Just as children need to learn the alphabet before they can learn how to spell words, your dog must learn basic obedience—"sit," "down," "come," and "stay"—before he can advance to any other type of training. Basic obe-dience is your dog's first step to becoming a good pet. The education

CHOOSING A DOG TRAINER

Especially if you are a first-time dog owner, formal obedience classes may be a good investment. Besides pro-viding much-needed training, obedience classes offer opportunities for socialization, help adopted dogs develop trust and con-fidence, and offer expert guidance for dog adopters. To determine whether a particu-lar canine education program is a good one, look for the following:

The program should use positive train-ing methods. Physical punishments and aversive (harsh) training methods are not appropriate in obedience training.

In the classes, the ratio of dogs to instructors and assistants should be no greater than eight to one.

The instructor should work well with people and dogs.

The instructor should be a member of a relevant professional organization, such as the Association of Pet Dog Trainers (APDT) or the National Association of Dog Obedience Instructors (NADOI).

FAST FACT

Most dogs don't respond well to anger, so be calm but firm when training your pet. Dogs can be trained because they want to please their human companions. With patience and consistent methods, your dog will learn the rules of the household and behave appropriately.

you give your adopted dog will last a lifetime, so invest the time to train him properly. Afterward, reinforce his skills occasionally to keep him in good practice.

Food rewards make it easy to teach your dog basic obedience. Once your dog has mastered a skill, however, you must begin to phase out the food rewards for that skill. Your dog, after all, must learn to obey without the incentive of food. Gradually diminish food rewards during training sessions by offering a treat every other time your dog performs a skill, then every three times, and so on, until food rewards are no longer necessary.

When food rewards are completely withdrawn, you must make it clear to your dog that you still expect him to obey. Use a firm voice, if necessary, to convey your authority and expectations. But bear in mind that adopted

dogs often take a few weeks to several months to trust and respect a new owner. Be patient with your adopted dog as he learns to transfer his devotion and loyalty to you. Soon, he will obey you simply because he has a desire to please you.

Teach your dog the "sit" command by holding a treat over his head and slowly moving the treat toward his back. As your dog lifts his head and backs up to keep his eye on the treat, he may drop his rear end into a sitting position. If he does, praise your dog and give him the treat. The next time, say "sit" when performing this maneuver so he can begin to associate the command with the behavior.

After the "sit" command, you can teach your dog the "down" command. With your dog in a sitting position, encourage him to lie down by holding a treat on the floor in front of him and drawing it slowly away from him. If your dog lowers his front end as he stretches out to get the treat, praise him and give him the treat. Practice getting your dog to stretch out more and more until he finally drops his front end all the way to the ground. When your dog has reached this point, you can begin to use the "down" command so your dog can associate it with the behavior.

"Come" is a basic obedience command that you should practice as often and in as many places as possible. Encourage your dog to come when you call by slapping your thighs, clapping your hands, or running away from your dog to entice him to chase you. Reward your dog with a treat each time he complies. Until your dog responds reliably to the "come" command, always take precautions to prevent him from bolting. Keep your dog in a fenced area or on a leash whenever outdoors.

To teach the "stay" command, you need to begin with short practice durations and with minimal distance between you and your pooch. With your dog in a sitting position, say, "Stay." Then take one step away from him. Step back toward your dog immediately and reward him with a treat if he maintained his sitting position. After your dog stays consistently when you take one step away from him, try taking two steps, then three steps, and so on, until you can cross the entire room with your dog remaining firmly seated.

PROBLEM BEHAVIORS

Rarely is there a dog, adopted or otherwise, that doesn't challenge its owner with a problem behavior or two. The trick to solving a problem behavior is first to determine why the dog is acting that way. Dogs that soil the house or destroy things when their owners are gone may suffer from boredom or separation anxiety. In either case, a food-stuffed toy or an occasional date at the local doggy day care facility should help keep the dog occupied and stimulated. A dog experiencing separation anxiety might feel more secure in a crate or exercise pen, which can be like a den.

Problem behaviors are often a dog's expression of unhappiness. Maybe the dog needs more exercise. Maybe the dog needs more human attention or a doggy playmate to fulfill his need for companionship. Be patient with younger dogs that have not yet acquired the self-control they will gain from maturity. The shelter experience can be traumatic for some adopted dogs, and some of them suffer from insecurity. Be sure to give your dog time to heal and feel secure in his new home.

Fortunately, the great majority of problem behaviors are solvable. If you feel particularly frustrated with a problem behavior, however, don't hesitate to seek professional advice. Your adoption agency may have a canine behaviorist on staff who can assist you. With resourcefulness and persistence, you can mold just about any dog into the pet of your dreams.

CHAPTER THREE

Adopting a Cat

If you think cuddly kitties make awesome pets, you're not alone. More than 37 million U.S. households include at least one pet cat, according to the American Veterinary Medical Association (AVMA). Why are cats so popular? There are many reasons. Cats are easy to keep. They demand less time and attention than dogs, they don't need to be confined to cages like rabbits or rodents, and most of them have meager grooming requirements. In addition, their small size and quiet, nondestructive nature make them good neighbors in just about any type of living situation. Combine these qualities with the fact that cats are purr-fectly affectionate,

According to the Humane Society of the United States, 22 percent of the 93.6 million pet cats currently living in the U.S. were adopted from an animal shelter.

and it's obvious why they have earned such a strong following.

CHOOSING THE RIGHT CAT

There is usually no shortage of cats waiting to be adopted. Although it's nice to have a large assortment from which to select your new feline friend, having too many choices can also pose a problem: How do you choose just one? You don't have to do that, of course. In fact, the average number of kitties per cat-owning household in America is 2.2, according to the AVMA. But to help you decide which kind of cat or cats would suit you the best, consider the various physical and temperamental characteristics of felines.

PHYSICAL CHARACTERISTICS: With regard to physical characteristics, there is far less variation in the feline world than in the canine world. All cats come in a practical size—adult females usually weigh in at 6 to 10 pounds (2.7 to 4.5 kg), adult males at 10 to 15 pounds (4.5 to 6.8 kg).

The most important physical difference among cats is length of hair. Long-haired cats are luxurious to the touch and glamorously attractive, but they do require more grooming attention. To prevent matting, their coats need to be brushed or combed daily. By contrast, a short-haired cat can keep its own coat groomed with its rough, rake-like feline tongue. So before you pick a kitty to adopt, decide whether you want to put the time and effort into maintaining a long-haired cat's plush exterior. If not, choose a short-haired, self-grooming feline.

Long-haired cats like this Persian require a lot of work to look this good.

Some cats and dogs get along famously, while others become mortal enemies. If you already have a dog, make sure it is "feline friendly" before adopting a cat. When in doubt, it's best to adopt a cat on a trial basis to make sure the animals will get along.

You should also be aware that long-haired cats are prone to experiencing havoc with hairballs. All cats get wads of hair in the stomach from grooming themselves. But whereas a short-haired feline can usually regurgitate or pass these hairballs through its digestive tract, a long-haired cat often cannot. Serious problems can result from this situation. If you adopt a long-haired kitty, you'll need to provide a regular dietary supplement to help your feline friend pass ingested hair.

PERSONALITY AND TEMPERAMENT:
Some of the biggest temperamental differences between cats are gender related. Males tend to be more boisterous than females. They are outgoing and quite solicitous of human attention. Females, on the other hand, are often more reserved, sensitive, gentle, and independent.

Of course, there are always exceptions to these generalizations. But if you want a cat that gives you a lot of attention, and if you don't mind a cat that expects a lot of attention in return, a male might be your best choice. If you're looking for a gentler, less demanding feline, a female might make you happier.

There are some breed-based differences in cat personalities. For example, Siamese tend to be especially vocal and outgoing. Persians are more likely to have a laid-back, lap-kitty disposition. As with mutts, it's often difficult to determine the ancestry of a mixed-breed cat. However, if a cat appears to share a lot of physical traits with a particular breed, it may also share some temperamental characteristics with that breed.

THE MULTIPLE-CAT HOUSEHOLD: Many people will attest that two or more cats are better than one. Cats make great companions for each other. Kittens, in particular, get into much less mischief if they have a kitty playmate to help them expend their energy. And of course, more cats means more love. Since a cat's food and care requirements aren't excessive, it isn't much more bother to have two cats instead of one. The most significant consideration is the additional veterinary expense.

Cats are much more social than most people realize. Still, they can be somewhat finicky about their feline friends. So if you are considering adopting two cats, your chance of finding compatible kitties is best if you adopt two kittens together or a bonded pair of adult cats. Bonded cats are those that have already

HEREDITARY ISSUES

The bond between cats and humans is an old one. Researchers believe that around 10,000 years ago, wildcats were drawn to early farming settlements in the Middle East. Because rats, mice, and other rodents proliferate where grain is stored, the wildcats were able to find abundant prey. And the farmers were naturally happy for the help in controlling the rodent population. The mutually beneficial relationship made the cat a natural for being domesticated.

After so many centuries living among and being bred by humans, today's domestic cat, Felis catus, displays much more variation than did its wild ancestors. Some of this variation is readily apparent. To the delight of cat lovers, F. catus comes in an abundance of color patterns. But human intervention in feline breeding has in some cases produced physical problems. Flat-faced cats like Persians often suffer breathing difficulties. The Scottish Fold, a breed of cat with folded ears, is prone to a degenerative joint disease called osteochondrodysplasia. And the Sphynx, a hairless breed, cannot tolerate temperature extremes and is at risk for sunburn and skin irritation. When choosing a cat, you should be aware of hereditary physical issues.

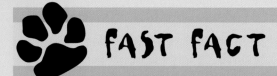

FAST FACT

Cats are highly susceptible to stress. To calm your adopted kitty and help her adjust to her new home, consider using a feline pheromone spray or diffuser. These products mimic the pleasurable pheromones cats produce from the glands on their heads. When your cat rubs the side of her head on you, she's marking you with these "friendly" pheromones.

established a close relationship with each other. Many shelters offer special adoption fees if you adopt your cats in pairs.

If you already have a pet cat and want to adopt a second one, choosing the right kitty companion for your existing pet can be a little trickier. In many cases, it is preferable to adopt a kitten, as kittens often awaken the nurturing instinct in adult cats. This can make your resident cat more receptive to the new feline family member.

Integrating another adult cat into your family isn't impossible. Adult cats can and do develop close relationships with each other, but their individual personalities must be compatible. A calm, friendly male cat might be more open to new feline relationships than a sensitive and

reclusive female. Adult cat pairings are most successful when both cats have amiable personalities and neither cat is dominant. When in doubt, it's best to do an adoption on a trial basis to make sure there are no serious personality conflicts.

PREPARING FOR YOUR NEW CAT

Cat keeping is a wonderful experience. You'll have purrs and kitty cuddles to look forward to every day. But you'll have to make some adjustments to your home and lifestyle to accommodate your feline friend. In addition to obtaining the supplies you'll need to care for your new cat, you'll have to put some effort into turning your home into a kitty kingdom.

SUPPLIES: One of the first things you might consider purchasing for your new cat is a collar. Be aware that cats are notorious for getting their collars snagged on things. To avoid a strangulation hazard, purchase a cat collar that has elastic, or fit your cat's collar loosely enough to permit her to escape in a pinch.

Unfortunately, these collar safety measures also make it very easy for cats to lose their collars. Because of this, you should consider getting an ID microchip for your feline.

When purchasing food and water bowls, keep your kitty happy by choosing low-sided bowls that won't scrunch her whiskers when she eats and drinks. Keep yourself happy by opting for something dishwasher safe and easy to clean. Since some cats have a habit of pushing their bowls around and spilling water on the floor, heavy or non-tip bowls are the best.

A litter box should also be waiting for your kitty when you bring her home. In fact, this is the first item you should show your new cat, so she knows exactly where to find it. Since some cats are very particular about their toilet facilities, you might want to start with an inexpensive pan-style litter box and plastic scooper until you become familiar with your cat's preferences. Scented litter can also

cause problems for some felines, so start with an unscented litter to ensure that your cat gets off on the right foot with litter box training.

The right scratching post is also very important, as it will help protect your furniture from claw damage. Choose a sturdy scratching post that is tall enough—at least 30 inches (76 cm)—and covered with a coarse material. If the post isn't tall enough, your cat won't be able to stretch when she scratches. If it isn't coarse enough, she won't be able to get enough resistance from it to shed the outer sheaths of her claws. A sisal rope or sisal fabric covering on the post is ideal.

Because you'll need something in which to transport your cat, a pet

If you don't provide a proper scratching post, your cat will turn to table legs or other furniture to keep her claws sharp.

carrier should also be on your list of necessary supplies. It's not safe to allow a cat to roam free inside a moving vehicle, as some cats aren't fond of car rides and can get stuck trying to hide under a seat or, heaven forbid, a brake pedal! Choose a pet carrier that offers some privacy for your cat. This will make her feel secure in it.

For keeping your cat's nails in manageable condition, you'll need a toenail clipper. The only other grooming necessity is a brush. For a short-haired cat, a soft rubber curry brush will do. A long-haired cat requires a brush that provides deeper coat penetration or a long-toothed comb.

Cats appreciate a soft place to nap, but the back of a couch or a bed pillow is just as appealing to them as a pet bed. If you do decide to splurge on a pet bed for your special kitty, place it in a high location with a good view if you want her to use it.

Finally, don't forget to invest in some stimulating toys. Toys will provide exercise and mental stimulation for your kitty, relieving stress and boredom. As important as they are for your cat's physical and mental health, cat toys are also a good source of entertainment for you. Who can resist watching a cat at play?

Cat treats are also a good thing to have on hand when your kitty comes home. Treats are not just for spoiling your favorite feline. You can use them to teach your cat to come when you call her name. This is always a good thing for a new kitty in a new home to learn.

TERRIFIC TOYS

Toys are important for your adopted cat's physical and mental health. Toys you might want to consider include:

A cat teaser, which consists of a toy attached to a stick with string. This is a great toy for interacting with your new pet.

Toys that encourage your cat to play by herself, like ball chasers and doorknob hangers. These can help keep your active kitty out of mischief.

Economical homemade toys, like a good old-fashioned paper bag in which your kitty can play peek-a-boo, or a cardboard box with a Ping Pong ball inside for your cat to bat around. These can provide exercise for your cat, as well as free entertainment for you.

MAKING YOUR HOME SAFE: Cats have a well-earned reputation for being curious. Their penchant for exploring small, dark spaces is what helps them find their rodent prey. Unfortunately, it also gets them into trouble sometimes. Kittens are especially naïve about potential hazards. Prevent your new cat from getting into a dangerous predicament by cat-proofing your home.

Some cats think electrical cords are just as much fun to play with as balls of yarn. If you cannot remove cords from your cat's environment, cover them or block them off so your cat can't get at them. Prevent your cat from playing behind your television set and electronics by arranging your furniture so that your cat can't access those areas.

Curious kitties sometimes explore with their mouths. Keep all household cleaners, detergents, and medications locked away or out of your cat's reach. Many houseplants are also toxic to cats if ingested. For a comprehensive list, visit the ASPCA Web site at www.aspca.org/pet-care/poison-control.

Cats love to play with stringy or dangly objects, but these could cause strangulation or, if ingested, an intestinal blockage. Always put your kitty's stringed toys away when you're not playing with them. Keep string, yarn, tinsel, and streamers away from your cat. Also, don't forget about pull strings on blinds, which are a favorite plaything for cats. You can find safety devices for these in the infant section of department stores.

Some of these precautions may turn out to be temporary. Your cat may show absolutely no interest in electrical cords, for example. The key is to observe your new kitty closely to determine which precautions you need to keep in place permanently.

LIVING ARRANGEMENTS: Your cat is a member of your household, and this means you'll have to make arrangements for where she will eat, sleep, and toilet. For feeding, choose a quiet spot where children and other pets won't disturb your cat. Her food should be in a separate area from her litter box, as cats don't enjoy eating in their bathrooms any more than humans do.

Cats are pretty good at choosing their own favorite spots for sleeping. If there are any areas where you don't want your kitty to bed down, make them off limits right away. You can use deterrents such as citrus-scented air fresheners or double-sided tape to discourage your cat from claiming an area as her own.

The amount you feed an adult cat should depend on her size and activity level.

CARING FOR YOUR NEW CAT

Nurturing a new cat can be very rewarding, as felines will let you know they appreciate what you do for them. Pleasing purrs and friendly head rubs are your cat's way of thanking you every time you feed her, groom her, or exercise her. Give your cat plenty to be happy about, and she'll pay you back with five times the affection!

FEEDING: Most commercially prepared cat foods provide a balanced diet with all the vitamins and minerals your cat needs to survive. But there's a difference between providing everything your cat needs to survive and providing everything your cat needs to be happy and healthy. Lower-quality cat foods contain inferior ingredients that can leave your cat with a dull coat, a low energy level, and poor immunity. High-quality cat foods will help keep your kitty looking, acting, and feeling her best.

Determining the quality of cat food is similar to determining the quality of dog food. Choose a cat food that lists fish, chicken, or another meat product first on the ingredients label. If the first ingredient is a meat by-product or a grain product, the food is not of a good quality. Also check the ingredients for the type of preservative the food contains. Look for natural preservatives like vitamin E ("mixed tocopherols") and vitamin C. Avoid artificial preservatives like BHA or BHT.

These characteristics of quality apply to any form of commercially prepared cat food—dry (kibble), wet (canned), or moist (pouched). Moist foods are the poorest choice for your cat's main fare because they contain additives to preserve their moistness. Nevertheless, it will certainly do no harm to give your cat a moist morsel now and then as a treat.

Dry foods offer the best value because they contain the highest amount of food product by volume. Unfortunately, cats don't concern themselves with domestic budgets. Felines are decidedly in favor of canned foods, the texture and flavor of which they find more appealing. But dry versus canned food need not be an either/or choice. You can benefit from dry food's affordability and still please your feline's refined palate by giving your pet a little of each.

GROOMING: Fastidious felines spend an awful lot of time grooming themselves. But a good brushing at least once a week will still benefit your cat's skin and coat health. It can also keep the shed cat hair in your house

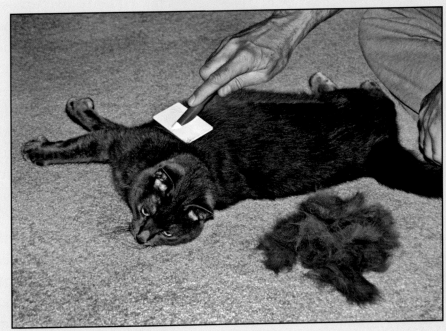

Occasional brushing will remove dead or loose hairs from your cat's coat and keep them off your rugs and furniture. Once a week should be plenty. However, brushing more often is fine, and your cat will appreciate the attention.

to a minimum. Most important, grooming can be a pleasurable bonding activity for you and your cat. Did you know that bonded cats often groom each other? Brushing your cat is one of the best ways to show your cat how much you love her.

Grooming should be a calm, gentle, leisurely activity, especially when it comes to nail trimming. The best time to clip your cat's nails is when she's just getting up from a nap and she's still a little tired. Cats that are in the mood for play generally don't have the patience to sit still long enough for this procedure.

Your adopted cat should rarely require a bath, but it's still a good idea to have bathing supplies on hand. Cats do occasionally get into sticky or oily things in the course of their explorations, and you don't want your pet to ingest such substances when she licks her fur. A gentle, tearless pet shampoo, along with a spray nozzle, sink mat, and towels, will help you bath your cat if this job becomes necessary.

EXERCISING: Cats are incredible athletes. They can jump heights equal to five times their body length. They have outstanding eye-paw coordination and lightning-fast reflexes. And, of course, they almost always land on their feet—even after an amazing jump or flip.

Your athletic feline needs opportunities to exercise. One fun way to give her a workout is to have her chase cat toys. You're guaranteed to be entertained.

But playing with your cat isn't the only way to exercise her. Many cats enjoy spending time outdoors. An outdoor pen or enclosure can allow your cat to get some fresh air and

Playing with your cat can provide good exercise for her and entertainment for you!

FAST FACT

Different cats react in completely different ways to certain stimuli. For example, catnip puts some cats into a state of euphoria, but has no apparent effect on other cats. Laser pointers excite the prey drive in some felines, yet others couldn't care less about the points of light.

exercise safely. If you introduce your cat to a collar and leash slowly, your cat may even learn to enjoy going for walks, especially during quiet times of the day. And, to give your kitty something to get excited about, don't forget to provide a new toy once in a while.

TRAINING YOUR CAT

Some people mistakenly assume that cats, because of their independent nature, are not trainable. This couldn't be further from the truth. You must train your cat if she is to be a good house pet. Cats never would have become such popular companions if they couldn't be trained to use a litter box and scratch post, or trained not to climb on the drapes or help themselves to the food on dinner tables. Reinforce good behaviors and discourage undesirable behaviors from the very beginning.

LITTER BOX TRAINING: Cats have a natural instinct to bury their waste, which makes it easy to convince them to use a litter box. In fact, litter box training involves proper management of your cat's toilet facilities more than it involves active training. Cats will always prefer to use an appropriate material like cat litter rather than have accidents in the house. So if a cat tends to "go outside the box," there's probably something wrong with the litter box.

If your adopted cat seems averse to using her litter box, the explanation may be one or a combination of the following:

- The litter is scented. Some cats are very sensitive to scented litter and refuse to use it. Try an unscented brand of litter.
- The cat is not neutered or spayed. Male cats, in particular, instinctually mark their territory with urine. Sterilization can help prevent this behavior.
- The litter box is covered or has liners. Some cats don't like the confines of a covered litter box. Others detest the noise or feel of litter box liners. Try using a plain litter box.
- The litter box is in a noisy or busy place. Cats like privacy when doing their business.

Move the litter box to a quieter but easily accessible spot.

- The litter box is too busy. If you have more than one cat, the rule of thumb is to provide one litter box per cat plus one extra box. This way, if a litter box is already in use, or one of the cats is territorial over a litter box, your cats will have enough "bathrooms" to choose from to avoid conflicts. Also, make sure the litter boxes aren't too close to each other, as territorial problems may extend over more than one litter box.
- The litter box is too dirty. Some cats won't use a litter box that is too soiled. A weekly litter box cleaning is fine for most cats, but some prefer a daily cleaning. Try cleaning your litter box more frequently.
- Your adopted cat is still adjusting to her new situation. Stress and a change in diet may contribute to diarrhea or constipation, and this may result in litter box lapses. Give your new cat a couple weeks to adjust to her new environment.
- Your cat may be sick. Urinary tract infections and obstructions are relatively common in cats. Have your cat examined by a veterinarian to rule out medical causes for her behavior.

Other things you can do to ensure that the litter box will receive your cat's approval include purchasing a litter box that is large enough and filling the litter to a proper depth. A litter box should measure at least 22 x 16 inches (56 x 41 cm). The litter should be about 2 inches (5 cm) deep. Although litter boxes come in dozens of styles—including self-cleaning models—and varying price ranges, your priority should always be to please your cat first and yourself second.

SCRATCHING-POST TRAINING: Training your cat is a matter of convincing your free-thinking feline that

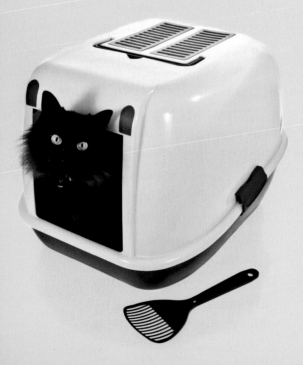

Most cats in shelters are there through no fault of their own. Often, cats and other pets are given up for adoption because of a change in their prior owner's life situation, rather than bad behavior on the pet's part. By taking a cat home from a shelter, you're saving that pet and making room so another pet can be saved as well.

she wants to do what you want her to do. This rule definitely applies to scratching-post training. Cats have to scratch on something, and when you provide them with the most awesome scratching material, they won't be very interested in scratching on anything else.

So what does a cat want in a scratching post? It should be at least 30 inches (76 cm) high, so that the kitty can stretch out completely. It should be sturdy, with a post that has a wide, stable base to prevent tipping. And it should have a coarse covering material such as sisal fabric. These features would be more than enough to keep kitty claws off human furniture if cats simply wanted something to maintain their claws. But scratch-ing is more than a way for cats to sharpen their prey-snaring tools.

Cats also scratch to mark their territory. If you really want your cat to use her scratching post, you'll have to place it in a prominent loca-tion where her scratch marks will adequately announce her presence. When you consider the height and location of couch ends, you can see why cats tend to target them for scratching. If your cat has already made a habit of scratching on a piece of furniture, place the scratching post in front of the furniture. This will help her transfer her scratching habit to the post.

Besides providing a scratch-worthy post, you can make the post more attractive by rubbing some catnip on it. It may only take a few weeks for your cat to completely abandon your furniture in favor of her post. If your cat needs a little more incentive to make the switch, try putting some double-sided tape on your furniture. The uncomfortable stickiness will make the furniture less desirable.

Cats are often opportunistic scratchers. They tend to go for whatever appropriate item is close at hand when they get the urge to scratch. Make it easy for your cat to do the right thing by providing plenty of appropriate scratching opportunities. A second scratching station in a convenient place will help. It needn't be a post, either. Scratching pads are also available. They can be mounted on a wall or placed flat on the floor. Keep all these options in mind. With management and training, any cat can learn to keep claws in their proper place.

MANNERS: Cats aren't born knowing how to behave in a human household. Without some training, they may get into dangerous situations, cause household damage, or become downright annoying. So teach your cat some basic rules of the house.

The easiest way to discourage

your cat from behaving in undesirable ways is to communicate your displeasure with a verbal cue. Since cats are sensitive to hissing sounds, a sharp "shhht!" will often get a cat's attention. Use this sound and clap your hands, if necessary, to shoo your cat out of forbidden areas, such as behind the television set or off the kitchen counters. With consistent reinforcement, your cat will learn where you do not want her to go.

Passive deterrents also work very well with cats. For example, if your kitty is fond of playing among the cords behind your computer, you could place a citrus-scented air freshener there. Cats don't like the smell of citrus, so your kitty will start avoiding the area. You could also purchase a cat-training aid that emits a hissing sound. These kinds of deterrents will help your feline learn on her own where she shouldn't go.

Living harmoniously with a cat can be difficult at times. But with patience, persistence, and a little bit of creative thinking, you can solve just about any feline behavioral problem that arises. However, if you ever find yourself completely stumped, consult with your pet adoption agency or an animal behaviorist.

CHAPTER FOUR

Adopting a Bird

Birds embody beauty and grace. They have inspired countless poets with their melodic songs, magnificent plumage, and mastery of the skies. Many bird species make good pets. Perhaps you've been thinking of enlivening your home with the sound, color, and companionship of a pet bird. You'll find a wide array of homeless birds available for adoption. But do you know what type of bird is right for you?

CHOOSING THE RIGHT BIRD

All birds possess beaks and feathers, but there are monumental differences in the care, attention, and living situations they demand. Consider

Parrots have high care requirements, and as a result many are left unwanted and displaced as they mature. Only a small percentage remain in their original homes for their entire lifetime.

the physical and temperamental characteristics of the various bird species before deciding on which style of avian will complement your style of life.

PHYSICAL CHARACTERISTICS: Birds come in a great assortment of sizes, and size is a good indicator of the amount of time and care a bird will require. Generally, large birds require more care and attention than small birds. Big birds eat more, make bigger messes, and demand more one-on-one time with their owners. They also require a considerable amount of space for their cages and perches. How much room can you afford your pet? How much time and energy do you have to care for, clean up after, and play with a feathered friend?

Large birds also tend to be louder. This is an important consideration if you live in an apartment or otherwise have neighbors in close proximity.

FAST FACT

Many adoptable parrots have a scraggly appearance because they have plucked out their own feathers. This behavior usually results from stress. Once placed in an appropriate environment, many plucked birds grow their feathers back.

Parrots, regardless of the species, are notorious noisemakers. But they also have the unique ability to mimic human speech. If you have your heart set on a "talking" bird but want to minimize the noise, choose a smaller species like the budgerigar (parakeet) or cockatiel. While their repertoire won't be as large as that of an African Grey parrot or a Scarlet Macaw, they can be taught a few words. If you're willing to trade talking for the musical chirps of a songbird, you'll find a variety of finches that fit the bill. If you want a bird that's both quiet and fairly large, the soft-cooing dove might be just the ticket.

PERSONALITY AND TEMPERAMENT: The temperamental traits of birds vary widely by species. The one thing all pet birds have in common is that they are prey animals. This will be a concern for you if you already have pets with predatory backgrounds. Being natural enemies doesn't guarantee animosity between animals, but it does mean you'll have to evaluate your pets carefully to make sure they get along.

A cat or dog may have little interest in a large parrot, which is big enough to hold its own. But if a bird excites a predator's prey drive, it will make for a very stressful environ-

Zebra finches are hardy and relatively easy to care for, making them a good choice for a first-time bird owner. They are active and fun to watch, but don't make a lot of noise. Finches are very social birds, however, and should be kept in pairs.

ment for both. The bird will live in constant fear, and the predator will live in a constant state of arousal.

Whether birds like the company of their own kind depends on the species. Many small birds are quite sociable with each other, which may allow you to cage several varieties together. Smaller parrots, like parakeets and cockatiels, enjoy the company of their own kind. But larger parrots occasionally don't get along with each other.

Sociability with humans is often largely dependent on the bird's early experiences. Hand-reared birds—birds that were hand-fed by humans from a very young age—have great affinity for people. Birds raised by their parents, on the other hand, are naturally fearful of people. These birds can still be trained, provided the training begins while they are still relatively young, but it will take much more time and effort. If a bird readily perches on your finger or arm and allows you to stroke its head, it was probably hand reared.

PREPARING FOR YOUR NEW BIRD

Birds don't have the same capacity to wreak havoc in a house as do dogs or cats. But you'll still need to prepare for an avian arrival. Your new bird will require a proper habitat.

SUPPLIES: A birdcage can be more than a confinement space for your bird. It can be an integral part of your household furnishings. It's fine to choose a birdcage that makes an attractive showcase for your precious pet. But don't forget its primary purpose: to provide your bird with an appropriate living environment. Make sure the cage is large enough for the bird you have chosen. When in doubt, remember that bigger is always better. A large macaw will need a cage that offers at least 20 square feet (1.85 sq meters) of living space. Even the most diminutive finch would appreciate at least 2 square feet (0.185 sq meters) to spread its wings.

Your bird's cage will need some type of lining or bedding to catch your bird's droppings. Among enthusiasts, the best type of bedding is a topic of much discussion. Corncob bedding, cat litter, and cedar shavings should definitely be avoided. These materials can be toxic or can cause digestive obstructions if ingested by a bird. Safer alternatives include commercially manufactured bedding made especially for birds, which can pass safely through a bird's digestive system if eaten, and paper products such as unprinted paper, paper towels, and paper birdcage liners.

You'll need to furnish your pet's living quarters with perches, toys, and feed dishes. Choose perches that are an appropriate diameter for the size of your bird. Perches that are too large or too small will cause sore feet for birds as surely as ill-fitting shoes cause sore feet for humans. Be prepared to clean or replace your pet's perches occasionally as they get soiled.

If you have more than one bird in a cage, you'll need to provide more than one feed dish. Larger birds that subsist on a diet of both commercial mix and fresh foods should have separate dishes for these foods. A separate dish for water will also be required, and you should refill it with fresh water every day.

Parrots are very intelligent, and without some diversions they get bored. Fortunately, they are fond of toys, and many intriguing types are available. Make sure your parrot's cage always contains some toys to keep him occupied. But don't overdo it. Clutter can prevent your bird from spreading his wings—something he also needs to do periodically.

Besides providing a source of exercise and fun, some wooden chew toys will help keep your parrot's beak trim. It's important to give your parrot enough opportunities to wear down his beak so it doesn't become overgrown. A mineral block (for larger parrots) or cuttlebone (for budgerigars and cockatiels) can also help with this while also providing essential dietary components.

Another supplemental item you may need to furnish in your pet's cage is grit. Since birds don't have teeth and cannot chew their food, the consumption of grit helps to break down the food they eat. Most experts now agree that captive parrots on a good diet don't require grit. But some birds, like doves and finches, may still benefit from a source of grit. Research the diet requirements for your particular bird species before deciding to supply grit for your pet.

MAKING YOUR HOME SAFE: Most species of pet bird enjoy spending some time outside their cages, and a little bit of freedom can provide good opportunities for exercise. Keep your bird's activity time from turning into accident time by giving your bird a safe place to play. If you have an untrained bird that doesn't come to your hand or a perch when called, choose a closed room to let your little flyer out of the cage. This way, it will be easy to catch him when it's time to go back in the cage.

Parrots and other birds entertain themselves with toys. Chewing on wooden toys helps a parrot to keep its beak in proper condition.

Keep predator pets out of the room until you have a better idea of how they will react to your "unleashed" bird. The fluttering wings of a bird excite the prey drive in many dogs and cats. And it should go without saying that you should close all the windows in your bird's exercise room to prevent your pet from escaping.

Because of the bird's flight capabilities, it isn't always possible to make a room entirely safe. Be observant. Find out what kinds of hazards

If you own a cat, take steps to make sure that your bird will feel safe and will be secure in your home.

attract your particular bird. If your bird tends to nibble on the wires of a hanging light, for instance, you may need to cover the wire. Most birds eventually choose a favorite perch in the room, where they feel safe and can observe the world around them. Once your bird has established his favorite roost, you might want to put some strategically placed newspaper underneath to catch any droppings.

A larger parrot is often most comfortable on its own perch stand. Parrot cages sometimes come with a perch on the top. You can also purchase a freestanding perch. Choose a perch with a diameter that allows your parrot to curl his toes around the sides of the perch without curling under it. This will give him the best grip without fatiguing his feet. A few toys or treats by the perch will teach your parrot to enjoy his own personal platform.

LIVING ARRANGEMENTS: Finding an appropriate place for your bird's cage isn't just a matter of putting it wherever you happen to have room. Except for the very smallest, most pet birds can be exceptionally noisy and don't make very good bedroom companions. Choose a location where your bird won't disturb you at night and, if necessary, use a cage cover to calm your bird at bedtime.

You also need to find a place that is dry, free of drafts, and out of direct sunlight. While smaller birds prefer a bright but quiet corner where they can feel safe, larger birds often prefer a more central location where they can be a part of the daily activities in a household.

You'll also want to choose an area that is easy to keep clean. For all their wonderful qualities, birds are messy. Seeds and droppings are bound to escape your pet's cage. If you choose to put your pet's domicile in a carpeted area, a plastic floor mat under the cage will help tremendously with cleanup.

CARING FOR YOUR NEW BIRD

Birds can be gloriously resplendent, but it is the quality of care they receive that makes them that way. If you want your bird to have shiny plumage, a cheery attitude, and plenty of energy, give him everything he needs to be happy. A proper diet, regular grooming, daily exercise, and a clean environment will keep your pet bird in optimum condition.

FEEDING: The most common cause of ill health in birds is poor diet. Many adoptable birds come from homes in which they didn't get proper food or good care. Ideally, the pet adoption agency will already have helped your bird adjust to a healthful diet. Find out what type of food the agency has been feeding your bird, and obtain a supply of it. If you want to change brands, do so gradually by replacing some of the old mix with the new mix over the course of a week or more. If you need to introduce your bird to fresh foods, do this gradually as well.

Parrots require a large variety of diet components, including fats, calcium, and protein, as well as vitamins and minerals. Some perishable foods appropriate for parrots include cheese, apples, pears, bananas, carrots, celery, and oranges. Provide

A balanced diet is important for your pet bird's health. The nutritional needs of different types of birds vary, but most can be fed a combination of seeds, commercial pellets, and fruits or vegetables.

fresh foods in appropriate amounts to avoid health or digestive problems. Your bird is likely to favor certain foods, but too much of any one type of food will result in an unbalanced diet.

All birds, whether they require fresh foods or not, need to receive a commercial feed mix formulated especially for their species. This may include food pellets, seeds, and nuts. Investigate the specific dietary requirements for your particular bird, as it is dangerous to assume that all birds eat the same type of food. Parrots may need a vitamin supplement added to their food or water. (More information on nutrition for various types of birds is available at http://edis.ifas.ufl.edu/vm067.)

GROOMING: Birds are fastidious creatures that spend a great amount of time preening. So how much help could a bird possibly need in grooming? In the wild, birds have everything they need to maintain their unique vestments, and their lifestyle contributes to good hygiene. The activities of domestic birds, on the other hand, are much more restricted. Pet birds don't have the same opportunities to wear down their nails and beaks, nor can they bathe in puddles as their wild cousins do.

Nail trimming is easy to perform with a regular toenail clipper. With your bird on a wide-diameter perch, slip the clipper under each nail to trim off the tip. Be careful not to cut the nail too short, as cutting into the "quick" that supplies blood to the

Canaries sport pretty plumage and have a delightful song. Males are more popular as pets because they sing better and are more brightly colored.

FAST FACT

The purpose of nail trimming is to avoid foot problems caused by overgrown nails. For smaller birds, sandpaper-like perch covers can help to wear nails down more naturally.

nail will result in pain and bleeding. The quick in a bird's nail is much longer than the quick in a dog's or cat's nail, so be careful to trim only the very tip. A treat to keep your bird busy and distracted will help during this process.

Make sure your bird has mineral block, cuttlebone, or wood toys in his cage to help maintain his beak. Unless your bird has a beak defect or health condition, beak trimming shouldn't be necessary. But in any case, you shouldn't attempt to do this on your own, as an incorrectly trimmed beak can cause eating problems that may ultimately result in starvation. If your bird drops a lot of food or has difficulty eating, have your veterinarian or an avian expert check the bird's beak.

Your bird may seem perfectly capable of caring for his own feathers, but all the preening in the world cannot replace a bath. Bathing in clean water helps remove dirt and

excess oil from your pet's plumage. Some birds relish having a shallow pan of water to frolic in once a week, while other birds enjoy the spray of a water bottle. There are also bird sprays available for this purpose. Allow your bird some out-of-cage activity time to help him dry off after a bath. Some birds will tolerate a hair dryer on a low heat setting.

EXERCISING: Fitness is as much a part of your bird's health as is diet. One of the ways to ensure that your bird gets enough exercise is to provide as large a cage as possible, especially if your bird spends the majority of his time confined. Toys will help encourage your bird to be active. Always leave your bird's favorite toys available to him, but rotate the other

FAST FACT

If you notice feathers accumulating on the floor of your bird's cage, don't be alarmed. Birds molt about once a year. This is a gradual process during which birds lose a large number of feathers over the course of several months. Although your bird may appear somewhat ragged during this period, his ability to fly will not be impaired, and his splendid attire will grow back in due time.

toys or purchase a new toy for your pet once in a while. The novelty of new items will keep your bird physically and mentally stimulated.

Parrots and other hand-tamed birds require daily attention from their owners. Playing with your bird provides exercise for your winged friend. But it also does much more. It helps keep your bird accustomed to handling, meets his need for attention, and helps him develop trust in you. Set aside some time every day for bird play.

CAGE CLEANING: Keeping your bird's environment clean is vital to maintaining his health. A dirty bird-cage can be a breeding ground for bacteria. Depending on the size of your bird, you'll have to clean the cage anywhere from once a day to once a week.

In addition to the frequent replacement of cage bedding or liners, you should give the cage a thorough scrubbing at least once every three months. This includes scraping or replacing the perches, scrubbing the bars of the cage, and thoroughly washing your pet's food receptacles and toys. Don't use harsh cleaning products, as birds are very sensitive to chemicals. Use only hot water or a cleaning product made specifically for disinfecting birdcages.

GROUNDING YOUR BIRD

During out-of-cage playtime, your pet bird can get into trouble by flying somewhere he doesn't belong. Before you take the bird out, make sure outside doors are closed, overhead fans are off, and there are no hot surfaces that your bird can reach, such as a stove, a space heater, or a clothes iron. Even if you take these precautions, however, your winged pal could get hurt by flying into a window. That's because birds have difficulty seeing glass.

For the sake of safety, some avian enthusiasts recommend clipping pet birds' wings. Other bird keepers, though, don't believe in this practice. If you decide to clip, have your veterinarian or an experienced bird owner show you the proper technique, which involves trimming flight feathers. A bird that has been clipped correctly can fly short distances and thus won't get hurt dropping off a perch. You'll need to trim the feathers periodically, as they do grow back.

You can begin training a pet bird by feeding him seeds from your hand.

TRAINING YOUR BIRD

Birds are delightful companions because they possess both beauty and brains. They are pleasing to look at and fun to train. You would be missing out on one of the greatest joys of bird ownership if you didn't experiment with teaching your pet a few tricks to impress your friends. The foundation of all bird training is trust. Before you can teach your winged buddy anything else, you must first teach him to trust you.

HANDLING AND TAMING: Birds that are hand-fed by humans from infancy grow to have a high level of comfort with people. If your bird wasn't hand-fed, however, you'll have to take the time to tame him. Begin by offering your bird an especially delectable treat from your fingers. When your bird becomes comfortable munching on a treat held in your hand, use your other hand to begin stroking his back gently. Soon, your bird will learn that your hands mean no harm and that they actually bring good things.

You can then start teaching your bird to perch on a stick by holding a dowel inside your pet's cage and gently pressing it against the front of your bird's chest by his legs. This will push your bird slightly off balance, and he will step forward onto the perch. Get your bird used to this portable perch by moving it about the cage. Later, you can introduce your finger in place of the stick. When your bird is comfortable with your finger, graduate to taking him out of the cage. Work on taming your bird daily. The more handling your bird receives, the tamer he'll become.

Birds that are patiently tamed will be unlikely to bite. But if your adopted bird developed this bad habit before you got him, you'll have to address the behavior. Most parrots

The Blue and Gold Macaw is one of several types of birds that can be taught to mimic human speech. Like most other birds, Macaws enjoy the company of their own kind, but a bird that is distracted by a winged buddy may be less likely to talk. If you want to increase your chances of having a talking bird, adopt a single bird and give it lots of attention.

enjoy human attention, especially when it involves toys and treats. So when your parrot bites, say, "No!" sternly and put him back in his cage for a couple minutes. If such "time-outs" aren't effective, consult with an expert in bird behavior. Your bird's adoption agency may be a good source of behavioral advice.

SPEECH TRAINING: Parrots can do one thing better than any other domestic creature: they can imitate human speech. To develop this unique talent in your bird, choose a quiet time of the day, preferably morning or evening, when your bird is calm and it is easier to keep his attention. Most birds learn best without the distraction of other birds around. Begin with a simple word, like "hello," and repeat the word numerous times, pronouncing it clearly. You might notice your bird cocking his head and observing every movement of your mouth and lips. This is a good indication he is figuring things out. Even so, it can take several weeks or even months before your parrot will issue his first word.

Once your bird has learned his first word, you can begin adding more words and phrases, one at a time. Some trainers use food rewards to teach birds to talk. If you do this,

Budgerigars are intelligent, social animals that can be taught to speak, whistle tunes, play with humans, and do simple tricks.

make sure you deliver the reward immediately after your bird says the word you're practicing. Otherwise, he won't associate the reward with the talking. And when you're thinking of new and fun things to teach your bird, don't forget that birds are great whistlers and singers, too. The possibilities are endless.

CHAPTER five

Adopting a Small Mammal

Small mammals can make excellent, easy-care companions, but the definition of "small" is rather subjective. Some rabbits, which are from the scientific order Lagomorpha, can be larger than cats. On the other hand, animals from the order Rodentia, like mice, hamsters, and rats, are small enough to fit in the palm of your hand. In general, animals that fall within the "pocket pet" category are cute, fun, and economical to keep. They do, however,

have different needs than other pets. Before you let your heart fall hopelessly in love with a fuzzy little critter, find out what kind of pint-sized pet is right for you.

CHOOSING THE RIGHT SMALL MAMMAL

There are lots of small mammals from which to choose—the perennially popular hamster, the petite mouse, the dainty gerbil, the engaging Guinea pig (cavy), the intelligent

Rabbits, hamsters, and Guinea pigs are a few of the small mammals that can make great pets.

rat, the spirited rabbit, and even such exotic creatures as ferrets and chinchillas. You might be surprised to learn how many small, furry critters await adoption in animal shelters. Choosing a pet from such a wide array takes a little forethought, as you want to make sure the physical and temperamental characteristics of the species are right for your situation.

PHYSICAL CHARACTERISTICS:

Small-mammal pets can range in size from 2 ounces (57 grams) to 20 pounds (9 kg). A larger size means the animal will require a larger living area. Rabbits, Guinea pigs, and ferrets require sizable cages that can take up a significant amount of space. In addition, they need to get out of their cages regularly to get adequate exercise. Do you have a safe room in which you can let your

FAST FACT

Here's the life expectancy for several different small-mammal pets:

Rabbit	8–12 years
Guinea pig	5–7 years
Chinchilla	15–20 years
Ferret	7–10 years
Rat	2–4 years
Hamster	2–3 years
Gerbil	4–5 years
Mouse	1–2 years

furry buddy out to play?

Size is also a good indication of how much you'll need to invest in health care for your pet. Bigger pets tend to incur bigger veterinary expenses. Fortunately, most small mammals don't require vaccinations. The ferret is the only small pet in the United States that routinely receives vaccinations (for distemper and rabies). For health and behavioral reasons, rabbits and ferrets both receive neuter/spay surgery. The scent glands of ferrets are also routinely removed. Ideally, your pet's adoption agency will already have attended to the necessary vaccinations and surgeries for your adopted pet.

Small pets can come with a variety of physical characteristics, including different color patterns and

FAST FACT

Rabbits and rodents produce cecotropes—a softer form of waste pellets—which they eat. This is not a sign of illness. Rather, it is a necessary part of their digestive process. Cecotropes provide certain nutrients the animals cannot obtain in any other way.

While most small mammals are perfectly self-sufficient as far as grooming is concerned, long-haired types—such as this Guinea pig—do require some human attention to keep their fur from getting matted or soiled.

different types of hair. There is sure to be a small animal to please your sense of aesthetics. But don't overlook the extra care requirements for long-haired varieties.

TEMPERAMENTAL CHARACTERISTICS: Many small mammals are prey animals, and this has a significant effect on temperament. Nature has programmed these animals to be on constant lookout for danger. They have a strong flight instinct, which causes them to run and seek refuge at the first sign of trouble. It's not unusual for rabbits and rodents to be frightened by loud noises and sudden movements.

Keep nature in mind when adopting a prey animal into a home that already has predator pets. Predators and prey animals that grow up together often learn to get along very well with each other. In other cases, household harmony will depend on the individual personalities of the animals. Always protect your prey species pets from harm or harassment.

Whether prey or predator, most small mammals seem to enjoy the company of their own kind. Individual personalities tend to play a role in how well a pair of animals will bond. Males of any species, however, do have a tendency to compete with each other. Finding a compatible friend for your small pet can make pet keeping a little less demanding, as pets can amuse and occupy one another. If you don't think you will have time for daily interaction with your pet, consider adopting more than one. The only small pet that is not suitable for same-species companionship is the hamster. Hamsters will get into serious battles with each other.

PREPARING FOR YOUR NEW PET

When you adopt a small pet, you agree to provide appropriate living accommodations and to care for the animal properly. In order to meet these obligations, you need to have the necessary supplies on hand. You also have to make the necessary adjustments in your home. The more thought and effort you put into your preparations, the more readily your new pet will adjust to its little niche in your household.

SUPPLIES: Housing is the most obvious concern, because you need somewhere to keep your furry fellow. Pet supply stores carry an abundance of cages for small pets. But how do you know which is the best choice for your particular critter? Different species of pets prefer different features in their living environments. There are also some general rules to keep in mind.

Choose something that is durable and easy to clean. Wood-framed cages are very attractive, but rabbits and rodents can do a significant amount of gnawing damage to them. If a metal cage strikes your fancy, choose one made with galvanized metal to prevent corrosion. Plastic cages offer great options in style and may provide the most durability and ease of care. For small rodents, an aquarium with a cover can provide a secure living space with lots of visibility for observation.

Some animals enjoy a little vertical space in their enclosures. Chinchillas, which originated in the

Chinchillas will look for places to climb.

Andes Mountains, love to climb and hop on various levels of their enclosures. Ferrets, too, enjoy having different levels of their cages to explore—their wild ancestors prowled rabbit warrens. The more closely you can duplicate your pet's natural habitat, the happier your pet will be.

While cages with mesh floors are easier to clean and may be suitable for a rabbit's fur-padded feet, they can make the bare-padded feet of Guinea pigs and ferrets sore. Soft cage bedding provides the best footing for most small pets. Bedding comes in many forms, including sawdust, wood shavings, and ground corncobs. Check the packaging to make sure a particular form of bedding is safe for your species of pet.

To furnish your new pet's home, you'll need to provide a place to sleep, toys or exercise equipment, and food and water sources. Like people, pets prefer a quiet place to retire. A wooden nest box can make a cozy little bedroom for your pet. It will also provide your pet with a place to hide, which small prey mammals need to feel secure when they become frightened.

Toys and exercise equipment may include an exercise wheel, tunnels, a climbing apparatus, and wood chew items. Provide plenty of options to keep your pet busy. But leave enough room so that your pet can move around the cage. Chewing materials are important for rabbits and rodents. You can buy wood

Although some people think rabbits make ideal pets for children, this is not the case. Rabbits require gentle handling and a quiet environment. They can easily be startled and stressed by the loud noises and fast movements typical of excited children.

sticks or blocks from a pet supply store, or you can recycle cardboard products such as boxes or paper towel rolls. Just make sure the cardboard doesn't have printing on it, as some inks are toxic to small pets.

Supply your pet's food in a non-tipping bowl—stoneware or ceramic works well—or a container that attaches to the side of the cage. This will minimize the amount of food that is spilled or soiled. Since most small pets will quickly soak their bedding by playing in or tipping over a water bowl, it makes sense to use a water bottle instead. Small pets consume very little water, but you still need to replenish your pet's supply of fresh water every day. Bacteria will quickly multiply in a stagnant water bottle.

You may need to acquire supplies that are specific to your type of pet. Chinchillas require a dustpan for "bathing." Grooming tools may be required for long-haired pets. You might want to provide a hayrack in addition to a feed bowl for a rabbit or Guinea pig. Become familiar with the specific care requirements and supplies needed for your adopted pet. (More information on grooming and caring for various types of small mammals can be found at www.petfinder.com/pet-care/facts-small-mammals-pets.html.)

FAST FACT

Pet rabbits and rodents need plenty of appropriate chewing materials. Otherwise, their incisors, which grow continuously, will become too long.

MAKING YOUR HOME SAFE: Some small pets need playtime outside of their cages in order to get enough exercise and mental stimulation. In some cases, a large cardboard box, a puppy pen, or even a child's playpen with a few toys in it can suffice as a safe activity area for your rabbit, chinchilla, Guinea pig, or ferret. But if you want to give your furry little buddy more space, you can choose a room in your house to make pet proof.

Remove any hazardous substances, including potentially toxic houseplants that your pet may chew on. Cover or remove electrical cords and block off sensitive areas, such as behind your electronics and behind furniture and appliances where your pet might get stuck. Most important, never leave your small pet unsupervised in the house. Animals are very inquisitive, and there's no telling what kind of mischief your curious little companion will manufacture.

LIVING ARRANGEMENTS: Keep your pet's cage out of drafts and direct sunlight. An aquarium in a sunny location can quickly become a deadly hothouse. A cold, damp basement or a garage filled with auto exhaust fumes doesn't provide appropriate living conditions either. Instead, a quiet but visible location in your home is ideal, as this will allow you to observe and enjoy your pet, while your pet can feel like an important part of the household.

CARING FOR YOUR SMALL PET

One of the reasons you may have chosen to adopt a small mammal is that small pets are easy and economical to keep. They do, however, require a commitment of time and energy. When you care for your pet conscientiously, you contribute to your pet's good health and longevity.

This can mean a lot for animals like hamsters, gerbils, and mice, which have a relatively short life span of two to three years. So make every minute with your furry friend count, including the time you spend caring for your pet.

FEEDING: A proper diet for rabbits and rodents consists of three components: commercial feed, roughage (hay), and fresh food (grass, vegetables, and fruit). Commercial feed may come in pellet form or as a mix of pellets and grains. Because nutritional needs vary by species, it's important to purchase commercial feed formulated especially for your kind of pet.

Although nutritionally complete, commercially prepared foods are not a very good source of roughage, and they can contribute to constipation.

Like humans, Guinea pigs need to eat foods rich in Vitamin C to avoid health problems like scurvy. Feeding a Guinea pig leafy greens and vegetables along with commercial food pellets should meet his nutritional needs.

A hanging water bottle is much less likely to get knocked over and create a mess in your small mammal's cage.

To provide enough fiber, offer your rabbit or rodent an unlimited supply of hay, but choose good-quality grass hay like timothy. Alfalfa hay may be too rich and may cause diarrhea for small pets. Mixed hay may contain undesirable or even toxic plants. Many pet stores sell hay that is appropriate for small pets.

Fresh foods are a good source of vitamins, and your pet will welcome them enthusiastically. Grass clippings, dandelions, clover, broccoli, celery, cabbage, apples, and carrots are appropriate treats for most small pets. But there are a few important rules about feeding fresh foods to your pocket pet:

Always wash fresh foods before giving them to your pet. This will remove any pesticides or other contaminants.

Limit the amount of fresh foods you allow your pet to consume. Too much fresh food will surely cause diarrhea. If your pet has an outdoor pen, limit the amount of time you allow the pet to forage in the grass.

Remove uneaten fresh foods from your pet's cage. Fresh food can rot and mold in a short period of time. Cut grass will decompose quickly and become toxic.

Avoid foods with high water content, like iceberg lettuce and watermelon. These foods have little nutritional value and tend to cause diarrhea.

These diet suggestions do not apply to ferrets, which are obligate carnivores—meaning that meat must be their main source of nutrition in order for them to survive. In the past, it was common to feed kitten food or cat food to ferrets, as felines are also obligate carnivores. Today, however, commercially made ferret foods are available to meet the specific dietary requirements of this amiable member of the weasel family. Look for ferret food at your nearest pet supply store.

GROOMING: Most pocket-sized pets are self-grooming animals. So long as they live in clean cages, they are tidy little creatures. Some long-haired varieties of rabbits and Guinea pigs do require regular grooming attention, however. For these unique and glamorous varieties, brushing and combing are a necessary part of life.

You'll need to get your long-haired pet accustomed to such attention at a young age.

Such small, delicate creatures demand gentle grooming tools and a light hand. Rabbits have very thin skin that can easily suffer damage from rough hair treatment. Small pets also don't appreciate baths, so it's essential to keep their cages exceptionally clean to prevent soiling their fur. Spot cleaning with a damp cloth is usually all that is necessary to keep your pet's luxuriously long locks clean.

Even if your pet doesn't require regular hair care, many small pets—such as rabbits, Guinea pigs, ferrets, chinchillas, and rats—require regular nail trimming. Get your pet accustomed to this procedure by performing it regularly. A toenail clipper is

TREATS FOR TINY PETS

Do you want to win the heart of your new small pet? You can offer special treats. Be aware, though, that the following treats are appropriate for small pets in very limited amounts. Give your furry little friend no more than a few pieces per day.

Rabbits and Rodents: bananas, peas, grapes, raisins, sunflower seeds, apples, peaches, strawberries, raspberries, carrots, broccoli.

Ferrets: hardboiled or scrambled eggs, cooked and chopped meat (chicken, liver, beef, and turkey), baby-food meats.

Hamsters and other small rodents can use wheels to exercise inside their cages. Scientists have found that hamsters can run the equivalent of six miles or more in a single day.

usually sufficient to get the job done. Wrapping your pet in a towel may facilitate nail clipping by preventing your furry friend from beating a retreat.

EXERCISING: Larger caged pets such as rabbits, Guinea pigs, and ferrets need daily opportunities to get out of their cages to play. Some owners allow these types of pets to have the run of the house, much as you would allow a pet cat such freedom.

However, unless your house is exceptionally safe and you've gotten to know and trust your little companion, this may not be the best practice. It's always a good idea to supervise your loose pet.

Smaller creatures, like hamsters, gerbils, and mice, are quite content to spend the majority of their time in their cages—provided they can fulfill their exercise needs with exercise wheels, tunnels, gnawing materials, playtime with their owners, or ham-

Rabbits need larger areas to roam for exercise, but must always be supervised when out of their cages or hutches.

ster balls. A new toy or obstacle is always a welcome novelty that will stimulate your pet's curiosity and encourage activity.

CAGE CLEANING: Many people fail to realize how often a small pet's cage needs to be cleaned. A soiled cage can produce very unpleasant odors. Depending on the size of your pet, the size of the cage, and the type of bedding material you use, you'll need to clean your pet's cage every one to seven days. In general, larger pets require more frequent cage cleanings.

You might notice that your pet tends to soil the same area of the cage. This represents a natural "sanitation" instinct in animals. They generally don't like to soil their dens, burrows, or feeding areas. Pet owners often take advantage of this instinct to train their rabbits, ferrets, or Guinea pigs to use a litter box. This makes it possible to allow your pet a little more freedom in the house. It also makes cage cleaning easier.

TRAINING YOUR SMALL PET

Many people have successfully trained their small pets to respond to names or do tricks. This can be a great deal of fun, but chances are you'll first want to teach your pet two practical skills: how to use the litter box and how to tolerate handling. These skills will make everything about pet ownership more enjoyable.

LITTER BOX TRAINING: When training a rabbit, ferret, or Guinea pig to use a litter box, bear in mind that these animals are not cats. With these species, you might never achieve complete success. Be prepared to accept an occasional accident. Even so, many small pets become quite reliable, and this can make cleaning up after them considerably easier.

Start out with a sizable cage for your pet, as you'll need room for a small plastic litter box. Fill the litter box about one inch (2.5 cm) deep with litter material. For rabbits and Guinea pigs, make sure to use something other than clumping cat litter, which can cause intestinal blockages if ingested. Corncob bedding or shredded paper works well. Place the box in the part of the cage your pet tends to use as a toilet area. Also place a few of your pet's droppings in the litter box to encourage your pet to use it.

After your pet begins using the litter box consistently, take the box

Feeding a ferrett or other small mammal seeds from your hand will help him learn to trust you.

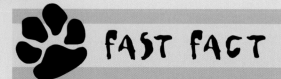

FAST FACT

Ferrets were originally domesticated—2,000 or more years ago—to assist in the hunting of rabbits and other ground-dwelling animals.

out of the cage when you take your pet out to play. At first, keep your pet in a small area outside the cage. As your pet becomes more reliable in using the litter box, you can expand the area in which your furry friend is allowed to roam. However, always keep the litter box in the same spot so your pet knows where to find it. Eventually, your pet will be able to enjoy much more space for out-of-cage play.

HANDLING: Nippiness is one of the biggest complaints of owners of small-mammal pets. No one likes to play with a pet that bites. Frequent handling is a must if you want your small mammal to tolerate your touch. Small pets generally don't bite out of aggression. Rather, a pet that is unaccustomed to handling may be scared or uncomfortable. Small animals may also bite out of curiosity, as they like to test things with their mouths.

If you have a small rodent, offer treats such as sunflower seeds in the palm of your hand. When your pet appears comfortable retrieving treats from your hand, begin petting your little friend. Gradually increase the amount of handling until your pet learns to trust you.

If you have a rabbit, you might want to wear gloves until the little nipper becomes more comfortable with handling. It's important not to immediately release a rabbit that has bitten you because this will only reinforce the biting behavior. Instead, wait until your rabbit is calm before putting the pet down. With patience and plenty of handling, most small pets learn to tolerate and even enjoy the attention they get from handling.

CHAPTER SIX

Adopting an Exotic Pet

Furred and feathered creatures aren't the only animals looking for new homes. Adoptable pets also come with scales, shells, slippery skin, and exoskeletons. If you want a pet that is a little different—yet remains fun to observe or hold—an exotic pet might be the perfect companion for you.

Exotic pets come in many different types. Adoptable amphibians include frogs, toads, salamanders, and newts. The reptile class features lizards, snakes, and tortoises. Invertebrates such as tarantulas, hermit crabs, and insects can also be kept as pets. Since reptiles are the exotics most commonly offered for adoption by animal shelters and rescue organizations, the information in this chapter will focus on them.

CHOOSING THE RIGHT EXOTIC PET

One of the most common misperceptions about exotic pets is that they lack personalities. Every boa con-

---

Lizards and other reptiles can make fascinating pets for young people.

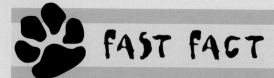

FAST FACT

Exotic pets are quiet. They won't disturb neighbors or housemates. They aren't emotionally dependent. They don't require constant care. All of this makes them excellent pets for people with demanding jobs or irregular work schedules. In addition, exotic pets are suitable for people who are allergic to cat or dog dander or to feathers. And they are generally economical and easy to keep. Most exotics require very little veterinary attention.

strictor, the thinking goes, will act the same as every other boa constrictor. A tortoise is a tortoise is a tortoise. One gecko is indistinguishable from the next. People with long experience keeping exotic pets know this isn't true. Like other animals, exotics display individual personality traits.

Might an exotic pet be for you? Carefully consider the characteristics of the various exotic species before making an adoption decision.

PHYSICAL CHARACTERISTICS AND SPECIAL CONSIDERATIONS: One of the most important physical characteristics you'll want to consider is size. Many reptiles are small and cute as juveniles, but they can grow

to enormous sizes. Be aware of the adult size of an exotic animal before making your choice, as large species require a great deal of space for their living environments.

Large snake species like the ball python and boa constrictor need sizable vivariums—aquariums outfitted as reptile habitats. Some tortoises grow to have a shell length of 30 inches (76 cm) and can weigh 100 pounds (45 kg). Tortoises require an exceptional amount of floor space for their habitat. Some enthusiasts construct their own "tortoise tables" to house their pets. How much of your living space can you give up for your pet's living space?

If space is a concern, there are many lizards that thrive just as much on vertical space as they do on horizontal space. Chameleons and water dragons are excellent climbers. Bearded dragons love to hang out in the branches of a taller vivarium, and their exceptionally docile temperaments make them popular as pets.

Besides space considerations, each species of reptile has its own special care requirements. For instance, each species requires a particular diet. Do you have the time to manually prepare a diet of fresh foods for a tortoise or iguana? Will it bother you to feed a snake thawed rats or mice? Are you prepared to feed your pet live crickets or meal-worms?

Exotic pets also require slightly different living environments. Although all reptiles are cold-blooded, which means they rely on their environment to regulate their body temperature, the exact conditions each requires is different. Some exotic pets come from arid climates. Others hail from tropical jungles. A heat lamp or heating pad will be necessary to provide your pet with a place to warm up, and a hiding rock will be necessary to give your pet a place to cool down. Thermostats or electrical timers may be necessary to provide just the right temperature conditions for your particular pet.

The humidity level in your pet's environment is also important. Humidity levels that are too high or too low can cause skin problems for reptiles. If you live in an area with extremely high or low humidity, you may need to monitor the humidity in your pet's environment.

The lighting in your pet's cage is another environmental concern. Many lizard species require unfiltered sunlight for proper bone development. In lieu of natural light, you'll have to outfit your pet's cage with artificial light that will provide the ultraviolet rays your pet needs.

Although most exotic pets are much easier to care for than dogs, some of them are still rather high maintenance. For example, it can take quite a bit of time to prepare the proper diet for a tortoise. Iguanas also require very specialized care and experienced handling. The time to become educated about your

Before bringing a snake into your home, make sure you won't get squeamish at feeding time. This corn snake is making a meal of a live mouse.

pet's needs is before you bring your exotic pet home.

TEMPERAMENTAL CHARACTERISTICS: Reptiles are independent creatures. They can thrive without human affection—and for some pet owners, this is a part of their appeal. If you're thinking of adopting a pet reptile, consider how much interaction you want with your pet. Do you want a pet that is easy to handle, or would you prefer to keep your hands off and just have a pet that is fun to observe? Do you want a pet that is appropriate for children?

Most gecko species are difficult or impossible to handle, as they can be fast and flighty. Other than the leopard gecko, which is slightly more docile, most geckos make colorful, active pets to observe. The green anole, another popular lizard species, is also a good pet to observe rather than handle.

If you want something more touchable, the

bearded dragon is one of the most popular lizards for first-time reptile owners. This amicable little creature—which reaches an adult length of about 20 inches (51 cm)—tames easily and will sit calmly on its owner's hand. Various chameleon species, too, will tolerate handling quite well.

Almost all snakes can adjust to handling. But because of their weight and strength, larger snakes are appropriate pets for adults only. Ball pythons, which can reach lengths of over 6 feet (1.8 meters), are a good choice for first-time owners of large snakes. Only experienced owners, however, should consider a boa constrictor. Boas commonly reach 10 to 15 feet (3 to 4.6 meters) long, and they have very sharp teeth.

Many smaller snake species make wonderful pets for responsible children. These include corn snakes, milk snakes, and rough green snakes. An adult should thoroughly tame any snake before allowing children to handle it.

Despite their high maintenance requirements, tortoises will interact more with their owners than will

Iguanas can be tamed, but they are often temperamental. They should only be handled by adults.

most reptile species. Tortoises tame easily and definitely make known their preferences in food and activities. Their interesting personalities make them delightful pets. Still, they don't enjoy a lot of handling. Tortoises are uncomfortable when their legs are suspended from the ground. They much prefer exploring the world from their own four feet.

PREPARING FOR YOUR EXOTIC PET

One of the most exciting aspects of adopting an exotic pet is preparing for its arrival. Assembling your pet's living environment is an important part of the exotic pet experience. When done right, your preparations will provide your pet with a safe, interesting habitat, in addition to allowing you to enjoy every aspect of exotic pet ownership.

SUPPLIES: In choosing an enclosure for your exotic pet, size is of course an important consideration. You must provide adequate space. But with reptiles, another vital considera-

SALMONELLA WARNING

Most reptiles carry the bacteria salmonella, which can infect humans and cause symptoms of diarrhea, fever, and abdominal pain. Infection is generally not serious for adults. However, children, the elderly, and people with compromised immune systems may experience serious health problems from salmonella. Take the following precautions:

- Don't adopt a reptile pet if there is a child under one year old in your household.
- Don't allow children under the age of five to handle reptiles.
- Require anyone who does handle reptiles to wash their hands with soap afterward.
- Keep vivariums and reptiles out of bathrooms and food preparation areas.
- Disinfect your reptile equipment on a regular basis.

You can create a nice habitat for an exotic pet inside a glass aquarium. This bearded dragon is warming himself in the glow of a heat lamp, which provides a warm area inside the habitat that he can use to raise his body temperature.

tion is security. Reptiles are notorious escape artists.

Aquariums make excellent homes for many types of exotic pets, as they provide wonderful visibility and are easy to clean. However, an aquarium must be fitted with a very secure screen top. Also available are glass enclosures with front doors made especially for exotic pets. While slightly more expensive than a typical aquarium, these are virtually escape proof.

Small, plastic cages are perfectly suitable for amphibians or invertebrates. But they generally aren't large enough for long-term reptile keeping. Some owners of exotic pets prefer to build their own animal habitats using wood, Plexiglas, and screening. A do-it-yourself cage can be a fun project that allows you to harness your creativity in designing a dream home for your pet. Be sure to keep in mind your pet's unique needs, however. For instance, wood is not an appropriate material to use for wet or humid habitats, as the wood may absorb moisture and warp.

Your pet's cage will need all the appliances necessary to provide the right lighting, temperature, and humidity for your particular exotic pet. But don't forget that it isn't just a cage; it's a habitat. You'll never regret putting a little extra effort into making your pet's home an attractive showcase. Constructing the habitat for an exotic pet is much like designing a zoo exhibit. You want to create an environment that is both pleasing to look at and natural for your pet.

Hide rocks, hollow logs, plastic plants, wood branches, and background scenery can provide visual interest as well as an enriching environment for your pet. You might even be able to find some of these items in your own backyard. Pebbles, rocks, gravel, branches, and dead leaves can add to the ambience of your display, provided they are clean and free of parasites or chemicals. You can be as extravagant as you'd like. Amenities such as electric waterfalls, rock walls, and live plants are available through retail or online sources.

The floor of your exotic pet's vivarium will also require covering material. If your pet is a desert species, sand would be appropriate. Pets that need to burrow prefer loam mixed with sand. Add some commercially manufactured "reptile grass" for a natural-looking feature that lizards and snakes can climb. Beware of cage bedding materials manufactured for other types of animals, as they may not be appropriate for exotic pets.

Other supplies you'll need to care for your new pet include a water bowl, food, vitamin and mineral supplements (depending on the species), a cage thermometer, a hygrometer (to monitor humidity, if necessary), and a spray bottle (to add humidity). As always, choose items appropriate for the size and species of your particular pet.

MAKING YOUR HOME SAFE: Many exotic pets become tame with frequent handling, but in order to handle your pet you'll need to take it out of its cage. Slow-moving tortoises are relatively easy to supervise, and their shells make it impossible for them to squeeze into small places. Snakes and lizards, on the other hand, can get into a considerable amount of trouble in the home if they escape their owners' hands.

When handling your snake or lizard, do it in a room that you have modified for safety. If you can, choose a room that has furniture on higher legs, so it will be easy to retrieve a pet that crawls under things. Cover heating vents and block the space under closed doors with towels. Close windows and check to make sure there are no small, dark places for your pet to hide. Make sure the floor is uncluttered, as you don't want your pet to climb on or ingest anything that might harm it. All of these steps will help ensure the safety of your pet and, in the event of an escape attempt, make it easier for you to catch the pet.

LIVING ARRANGEMENTS: Safety also applies to your pet's living arrangements. Keep pesticides and cleaning products away from your pet's vivarium. Also keep the vivarium out of direct sunlight. Although sunlight is good for the health of many reptile species, a vivarium in the sun can quickly become dangerously hot for its occupants.

For the same reason, don't locate your pet's vivarium too close to a heater or heating vent. It's also not a good idea to have a vivarium too close to a window or in another drafty area of your home. Put your pet's habitat in a spot where the room temperature remains fairly constant.

CARING FOR YOUR EXOTIC PET

With many exotic pets, the bulk of an owner's efforts go into setting up and maintaining a suitable habitat, as well as offering a healthful diet. Beyond that, many exotics don't need much care. They can get along just fine by themselves.

FEEDING: The diet and feeding habits of each exotic species is different, so you must become thoroughly educated in the nutritional needs of your particular pet. While some

CAPTIVE BRED VS. WILD CAUGHT

All pet reptiles were either bred in captivity or caught in the wild. Where an animal came from may have an influence on that animal's health and temperament. Breeders selectively breed reptiles in captivity to have docile temperaments and healthy traits. Wild-caught animals may be more skittish or aggressive. In addition, they may have acquired parasites from their wild habitats, and these can be the cause of unexpected death up to a year after capture. It may be impossi-

ble to tell whether an adoptable reptile was captive bred or caught in the wild. Before you adopt a reptile, have a vet check for parasites with a fecal test.

lizards enjoy mealworms for dinner, for example, others find these hard-skinned worms difficult to digest. You might need to dust your chameleon's food with a vitamin and mineral supplement. A young, growing tortoise might require a calcium supplement for healthy shell development.

Exotic pets fall into one of several categories: herbivores, which eat only plant material; omnivores, which eat both plants and animals; insectivores, which eat only insects; and carnivores, which eat only animals. Preparing meals for herbivores and omnivores is slightly more time-consuming because you must purchase and prepare a variety of fresh foods. Other dietary components are available in fresh, frozen, or canned forms.

Some exotic pet foods commonly available from pet supply outlets include live crickets, mealworms, waxworms, and locusts, as well as live or frozen mice and rats. Some exotics require two or three feedings per week, while others can go one to two weeks between meals. This, combined with the fact that many exotic pets are free fed, or allowed to feed at will, means that exotic pets are fairly self-sufficient.

Depending on the species of your pet, you might be able to find appropriate foods in your own backyard, including earthworms, snails, and

FAST FACT

Many exotic-pet experts recommend feeding pet snakes thawed frozen mice and rats rather than live mice and rats. Live mice and rats can seriously injure a snake that isn't hungry enough to devour them immediately. Snakes do not instinctually defend themselves against rodent attacks.

insects. But you should know that there is always a chance of bringing parasites or harmful bacteria into your pet's environment. If you want to play it safe, raise your own pet food or purchase it from a reputable pet store.

Many reptiles don't consume much water, fulfilling their hydration needs from the moisture content of their food. Nevertheless, it is essential that you provide your pet with a clean water source. Some exotic pets prefer a large water container in which they can wade. Others require only a small water receptacle. Still others prefer to drink droplets of water sprayed into their environments. Provide your pet with a species-appropriate water source, and, most important, change the water frequently to make sure it is clean and fresh.

OTHER NEEDS: With the right environment, exotic pets can take care of their own skin. The proper humidity level is critical for reptile skin health. Beyond that, a reptile only needs rocks, plants, or other objects against which it can rub during periods of skin sloughing. These objects help the reptile shed old skin.

Your exotic pet can take care of its own exercise needs as well. But again, the right environment is required. Provide your pet with a large enough enclosure—bigger is always better—with interesting furnishings. Various hiding places, climbing branches, and basking spots will encourage your pet to move around in the vivarium. If your pet doesn't have the opportunity to chase live food, place the food in different locations so that your pet has to search for its meals. And of course, human handling is a great activity for many exotic pets.

CAGE CLEANING: How often you should clean your exotic pet's cage will depend on the size and species of the pet, the size of the enclosure, and the type of flooring material. Generally, it's sufficient to perform a simple surface cleaning every week, and a thorough cleaning every few months. A major cleaning may involve completely replacing the flooring material and scrubbing or replacing cage furnishings. If you need to scrub your pet's vivarium, go to a pet store to get a cleaning product that is safe for your pet.

HANDLING YOUR EXOTIC PET

Although human handling isn't necessary for all exotic species, it is important for some. Large species, like boa constrictors and bigger monitor lizards, can become quite

When preparing a vivarium, include branches or other items for your pet snake to climb.

Children must be taught how to properly handle a pet lizard, like this leopard gecko, so that it isn't accidentally harmed.

unmanageable or even dangerous if they aren't accustomed to handling. Some smaller species of lizards and snakes just aren't as much fun if you can't handle them.

Frequent handling can keep your pet tame, but you also need to know how to handle your pet properly. Most animals don't enjoy having their body parts dangle. Large snakes, especially, are most comfortable when their owners provide adequate support for their weighty bodies. Tortoises are accustomed to having considerable pressure on their stout legs, and they are most comfortable if you carry them on a flat surface such as a board or storage box lid.

Lizards require careful handling as well. Many lizards dart around very quickly. It's tempting to catch them by the tail, but in so doing you can easily pull the tail off. Although a lost tail will eventually grow back, it's best to avoid inflicting this trauma on your pet. When catching your pet lizard, grasp gently near the head or use a net. With gentle, considerate handling, your exotic pet will learn to trust you and accept your handling. Then you can enjoy your pet in especially fulfilling ways, with close, hands-on experiences.

CHAPTER SEVEN

Responsible Pet Ownership

This is a great time to adopt an animal companion. There are more resources available to pet owners than ever before. You have the opportunity to benefit from decades of study and advancements in animal training, behavior, and health care. This is also a time of great awareness, with animal welfare taking a central place in the discussion of responsible pet ownership.

BECOMING AN EXPERT

The first thing you can do to promote responsible pet ownership is to become an expert on the species you plan to adopt. Read books, do research on the Internet, and talk to pet owners, breeders, veterinarians, and trainers. Knowledge is the first step to being able to care for and train your pet properly.

You might be surprised, on your

Providing proper veterinary care is an important aspect of pet ownership.

quest to learn as much as possible, that many of your previous ideas about pet ownership were wrong. Don't assume that because you had a dog as a child, you know everything you need to know about owning a dog. Over the years, there have been extraordinary advances in dog-training methods. There have been similar advances in the training of other pet species. For example, declawing surgery was once regarded as the only way to prevent a cat from scratching household furniture. Cat behavior studies have shown that belief to be mistaken. With training and the provision of proper scratching materials, felines can learn to avoid sharpening their claws on furniture.

PROVIDING HEALTH CARE FOR YOUR PET

Today, veterinary medicine incorporates advanced diagnostics and treatments that mirror those of human medical care. Veterinary specialties include ophthalmology, cardiology, and dentistry. Some veterinarians even specialize in alternative treatments, like herbal medicine, acupuncture, and chiropractic care.

Look for a veterinarian who has experience treating your type of pet, whether it's a chinchilla, a dog, or a reptile.

So how do you choose the right veterinarian for your particular pet?

FINDING A VETERINARIAN: You'll want to find a veterinarian who is experienced and knowledgeable in treating your species of pet, particularly if the animal you adopt is a less common type of pet. You may be able to obtain a referral to an appropriate vet from adoption agencies or breeders that specialize in your pet's species.

In addition to the appropriate experience, there are several factors you'll want to consider in choosing a vet. How far is the vet's office from your home? While you might be willing to drive a considerable distance to get your pet the best care available, is a potential vet close enough to handle emergencies? What are the veterinary hospital's hours of opera-

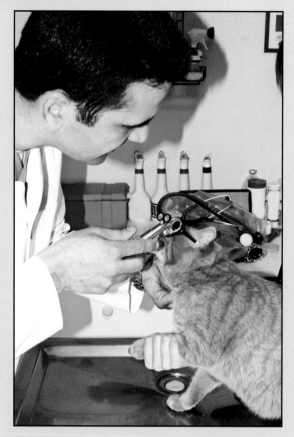

As a general rule, cats and dogs should have at least one veterinary exam every year.

tions, plan to evaluate that vet on an ongoing basis. Does the vet answer your questions adequately in language you can understand? Does the vet treat you and your pet with kindness and respect? Does the vet appear knowledgeable and competent? Your constant observations will help you develop a very important relationship with your veterinarian— one based on trust—or they may provide clues that it might be time to look for a new veterinary health care provider.

PREVENTIVE HEALTH CARE: The type of preventive health care your pet requires will depend on the pet's species. In general, cats and dogs require the most extensive preventive care, including vaccinations, annual checkups, sterilization surgeries, and health tests. This can result in significant health care expenses.

You can find vaccination guidelines for dogs at the American Animal Hospital Association Web site (www.aahanet.org), and for cats at the American Association of Feline Practitioners Web site (www.catvets.com). It is very important for your cat or dog to receive a number of "core" vaccines that will protect against highly contagious and potentially deadly diseases, such as panleukopenia virus (cats), canine

tion? If you work full time, you may want to find a veterinarian who offers evening or weekend hours. And what does the veterinarian charge for routine health care, such as vaccinations, checkups, or neuter and spay surgery? Be prepared to pay a little more at facilities that offer specialized diagnostic equipment and in-house laboratory services.

When you've found a veterinarian who appears to meet your expecta-

distemper (dogs), and rabies (both cats and dogs). Your veterinarian may also recommend certain "non-core" vaccines, depending on where you live and your pet's risk of infection.

KEEPING YOUR PET SAFE

Your duty to see to your pet's welfare goes beyond providing adequate health care. You also need to keep your pet safe. Pet proofing your home is an essential step in preventing accidents and injuries. But you can take the following steps as well:

Use a pet carrier when transporting your pet in a vehicle, as this will protect your pet in the event of an auto accident.

Keep your pet in a fenced area or on a leash when outdoors to prevent your pet from getting lost or getting into fights with other animals.

Never leave your pet outside unattended, as this could lead to the theft or loss of your pet.

Make sure your pet's outdoor enclosure is escape proof. Fences should be high enough and tight enough to prevent pets from jumping over or squeezing through. Outdoor pens for rabbits or Guinea pigs should have a mesh bottom to prevent pets from burrowing under them, and netting over the top to prevent predation by hawks.

FAST FACT

Some communities have adopted legislation that outlaws ownership of certain "dangerous" dog breeds, such as Pit Bulls and Rottweilers. Although many dogs of these breeds actually have excellent temperaments, check to make sure your community doesn't have a ban in place before you adopt one.

Check your pet's outdoor play areas for safety the same way you pet-proof your home. Sensitive or hazardous areas should be inaccessible to your pet.

Any pet that is be permitted to play outside should wear a collar with an ID tag in case he becomes lost.

Provide your pet with identification. A collar and ID tag can provide an instant form of identification for most cats and dogs, but a permanent form of identification is also a good idea. The microchip, a tiny data capsule that your veterinarian can inject under your pet's skin, is the most convenient and reliable form of permanent identification available. Although commonly used for cats and dogs, it is a useful identification tool for many other species as well, including rabbits, Guinea pigs, ferrets, birds, and even tortoises.

DEALING WITH PET OVERPOPULATION

The greatest problem affecting animal welfare today is pet overpopulation. You've already demonstrated your responsible attitude by giving a home to one of the millions of homeless pets. Through adoption, you've helped curb the demand for breeders to produce more pets. And, since most pet adoption agencies spay or neuter their animals prior to adoption, you'll avoid contributing to the pet overpopulation problem in the future.

You've certainly done your part. But consider doing a little bit more. Encourage others to adopt their pets and to have their pets neutered or spayed. If people embrace adoption as the preferred way to acquire a new pet, and if they see to it that their companion animals are sterilized, a day may come when pet overpopulation is no longer a major problem.

BEING CONSIDERATE

Pet ownership is not just about you and your pet. You are a member of a community. When you bring a pet into your life, your pet also becomes

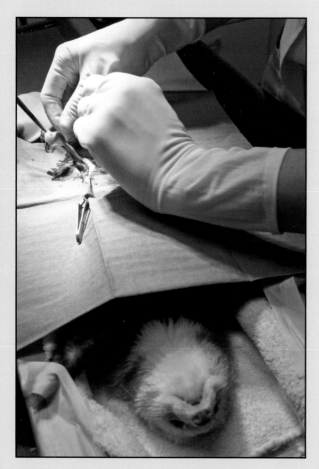

Even small mammals like ferrets can be spayed or neutered. This surgery helps to prevent unwanted pets.

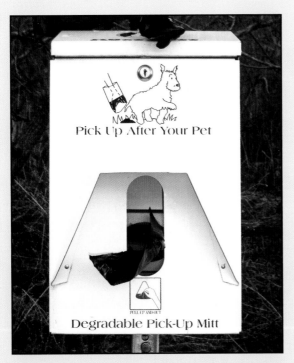

Show respect for others by cleaning up after your pet when in public. Not picking up your dog's waste during a walk could result in a fine.

a member of that community. In your role as a pet owner, make sure always to respect the rights of others.

Be considerate. Keep your pet off other people's property. Always clean up your pet's mess. Don't allow your pet to disturb neighbors with excessive noise.

You enjoy the company of your pet, but you can't expect everyone to feel the same way. Some people are fearful of animals. Others have serious allergies to animals. Always ask people if it's OK for your pet to approach them. Ask permission before you bring your pet to someone else's house. At your home, take your pet to another room if the animal appears to be making a guest uncomfortable.

When you respect other people's feelings, you'll help your pet fit into your community. You'll also become a good ambassador for pets in general. And, in addition to sharing your heart and home with a needy pet, that is one of the best gifts any animal lover can give.

Organizations to Contact

American Animal Hospital Association
12575 West Bayaud Ave.
Lakewood, CO 80228
Phone: 303-986-2800
Email: info@aahanet.org
Web site: www.aahanet.org

American Holistic Veterinary Medical Association (AHVMA)
2218 Old Emmorton Rd.
Bel Air, MD 21015
Phone: 410-569-0795
Web site: www.ahvma.org
Email: office@ahvma.org

American Humane Association
63 Inverness Dr. East
Englewood, CO 80112
Phone: 303-792-9900
Fax: 303-792-5333
Web site: www.americanhumane.org

American Society for the Prevention of Cruelty to Animals
424 East 92nd St.
New York, NY 10128
Phone: 212-876-7700
Web site: www.aspca.org
Email: information@aspca.org

American Veterinary Medical Association (AVMA)
1931 N. Meacham Rd., Suite 100
Schaumburg, IL 60173
Phone: 800-248-2862
Web site: www.avma.org
Email: avmainfo@avma.org

Association of Exotic Mammal Veterinarians (AEMV)
P.O. Box 396
Weare, NH 03281
Fax: 478-757-1315
Web site: www.aemv.org
Email: info@aemv.org

Association of Pet Dog Trainers
150 Executive Center Dr., Box 35
Greenville, SC 29615
Phone: 800-738-3647
Email: information@apdt.com
Web site: www.apdt.com

Association of Reptile and Amphibian Veterinarians (ARAV)
810 East 10th
P.O. Box 1897
Lawrence, KS 66044
Phone: 800-627-0326
Web site: www.arav.org

Canine Health Foundation
P.O. Box 37941
Raleigh, NC 27627-7941
Phone: 888-682-9696
Email: akcchf@akc.org
Web site: www.akcchf.org

Delta Society
875 124th Ave., NE, Suite 101
Bellevue, WA 98005
Phone: 425-226-7357
Email: info@deltasociety.org
Web site: www.deltasociety.org

House Rabbit Society (HRS)
148 Broadway
Richmond, CA 94804
Phone: 510-970-7575
Email: rabbit-center@rabbit.org
Web site: www.rabbit.org

The Humane Society of the U.S.
2100 L Street, NW
Washington, D.C. 20037
Phone: 202-452-1100
Web site: www.hsus.org

**National Association of
Professional Pet Sitters (NAPPS)**
17000 Commerce Parkway, Suite C
Mt. Laurel, NJ 08054
Phone: 856-439-0324
Email: napps@ahint.com
Web site: www.petsitters.org

**Orthopedic Foundation
for Animals (OFA)**
2300 East Nifong Boulevard
Columbia, MO 65201
Phone: 573-442-0418
Fax: 573-875-5073
Web site: www.offa.org

**Pet Industry
Joint Advisory Council**
1220 19th Street, NW Suite 400
Washington, DC 20036
Phone: 202-452-1525
Fax: 202-293-4377
Email: info@pijac.org
Web site: www.pijac.org

Pet Loss Support Hotline
College of Veterinary Medicine
Cornell University
Ithaca, NY 14853-6401
Phone: 607-253-3932
Web site: www.vet.cornell.edu/
public/petloss

**Pet Sitters
International (PSI)**
201 East King Street
King, NC 27021-9161
Phone: 336-983-9222
Fax: 336-983-9222
Email: info@petsit.com
Web site: www.petsit.com

Therapy Dogs International, Inc.
88 Bartley Road
Flanders, NJ 07836
Phone: 973-252-9800
Web site: www.tdi-dog.org

UK National Pet Register
74 North Albert Street, Dept 2
Fleetwood, Lancasterhire, FY7 6BJ
United Kingdom
Web site: www.nationalpetregister.org

Veterinary Medical Databases
1717 Philo Rd.
PO Box 3007
Urbana, IL 61803-3007
Phone: 217-693-4800
Email: cerf@vmdb.org
Web site: www.vmdb.org

Further Reading

Anastasi, Donna. *Gerbils: The Complete Guide to Gerbil Care*. Irvine, CA: Bowtie Press, 2005.

Athan, Mattie Sue. *The Second-Hand Parrot*. Hauppauge, NY: Barron's Educational Series, 2005.

Biniok, Janice. *Mixed-Breed Cats*. Pittsburgh: Eldorado Ink, 2010.

Bolan, Sandra. *Caring for Your Mutt*. Pittsburgh: Eldorado Ink, 2008.

Case, Russ. *Turtles and Tortoises* (Beginning Vivarium Systems). Laguna Hills, CA: Advanced Vivarium Systems, 2004.

Devers, Marie. *Turtles*. Pittsburgh: Eldorado Ink, 2009.

De Vosjoli, Philippe. *The Art of Keeping Snakes* (Herpetocultural Library). Laguna Hills, CA: Advanced Vivarium Systems, 2004.

Ducommun, Debbie. *Rats: Complete Care Guide*. Irvine, CA: Bowtie Press, 2002.

Fox, Sue. *Hamsters* (Animal Planet Pet Care Library). Neptune City, NJ: T.F.H. Publications, 2006.

Gewirtz, Elaine. *Fetch This Book! Train Your Dog to Do Almost Anything*. Pittsburgh: Eldorado Ink, 2010.

Harriman, Marinell. *The House Rabbit Handbook: How to Live with an Urban Rabbit*. 4th ed. Alameda, CA: Drollery Press, 2005.

Moore, Arden. *The Cat Behavior Answer Book: Practical Insights and Proven Solutions for Your Feline Questions*. North Adams, MA: Storey Publishing, 2007.

Purser, Philip. *Insect-Eating Lizards*. Neptune City, NJ: T.F.H. Publications, 2008.

Schilling, Kim. *Ferrets for Dummies*. Hoboken, NJ: Wiley Publishing, 2007.

Vanderlip, Sharon, DVM. *The Guinea Pig Handbook*. Hauppauge, NY: Barron's Educational Series, 2003.

———. *Mice* (Complete Pet Owners Manual). Hauppauge, NY: Barron's Educational Series, 2001.

Internet Resources

http://agsgerbils.org

The American Gerbil Society Web site is an excellent resource for gerbil fanciers.

www.afrma.org

The Web site of the American Fancy Rat and Mouse Association provides lots of valuable information for lovers of little rodents.

www.anapsid.org

Melissa Kaplan's Herp and Green Iguana Information Collection features a wealth of well-researched information on exotic pets.

www.aspca.org

Web site of the American Society for the Prevention of Cruelty to Animals.

www.catsinternational.org

If you have questions about cat behavior or how to train your cat, you can probably find the answers here.

www.ferretcentral.org

In addition to providing a list of ferret rescue groups, this site offers articles and answers to frequently asked questions about ferrets.

www.guineapigs.org

If you want to adopt a Guinea pig, this is the place to start. This site provides a list of Guinea pig rescue organizations by state.

www.parrots.org

The Web site of the World Parrot Trust includes an online encyclopedia of parrot species, links to parrot organizations, and beginners' guides to parrot ownership.

www.petfinder.com

This Web site, which features an extensive database of adoptable pets throughout the country, lists animal shelters by state.

www.rabbit.org

The House Rabbit Society Web site offers articles on rabbit care topics.

www.reptilechannel.org

The online portal for Reptiles magazine covers many topics of interest to the owners of snakes, reptiles, and other exotic pets.

www.tortoisetrust.org

The Tortise Trust Web site provides turtle owners with special updates and warnings about current problems in herpetology.

Index

Numbers in **bold italics** refer to captions.

Contributors

JANICE BINIOK has written numerous articles and books on companion animals, including other volumes in the OUR BEST FRIENDS series. A former professional dog groomer, Janice has over 30 years' experience with animals. She now combines her love of animals with her talent for writing to produce resources for pet owners. Janice has an English degree from the University of Wisconsin-Milwaukee and is a member of the Dog Writers Association of America and the Cat Writers' Association. She lives on a small farm in Waukesha, WI, with her husband, two sons, and a variety of animal companions. Visit her Web site at www.TheAnimalPen.com for more information.

Senior Consulting Editor **GARY KORSGAARD, DVM,** has had a long and distinguished career in veterinary medicine. After graduating from The Ohio State University's College of Veterinary Medicine in 1963, he spent two years as a captain in the Veterinary Corps of the U.S. Army. During that time he attended the Walter Reed Army Institute of Research and became Chief of the Veterinary Division for the Sixth Army Medical Laboratory at the Presidio, San Francisco.

In 1968 Dr. Korsgaard founded the Monte Vista Veterinary Hospital in Concord, California, where he practiced for 32 years as a small animal veterinarian. He is a past president of the Contra Costa Veterinary Association, and was one of the founding members of the Contra Costa Veterinary Emergency Clinic, serving as president and board member of that hospital for nearly 30 years.

Dr. Korsgaard retired in 2000. He enjoys golf, hiking, international travel, and spending time with his wife Susan and their three children and four grandchildren.